A Literary EDUCATION

—

Catherine Levison

CHAMPION PRESS, LTD.

Also by Catherine Levison

BOOKS
A Charlotte Mason Education
More Charlotte Mason Education

AUDIO TAPES
Balancing Act: to structure or not to structure
An Overview of the Charlotte Mason Method
History & Science
The Language Arts for (almost) Free

to order visit www.championpress.com

CHAMPION PRESS, LTD.
VANCOUVER, WASHINGTON

ISBN 1-891400-23-1
LCCN 2001086219

Manufactured in Canada 10 9 8 7 6 5 4 3 2 1

Cover photography by Gayle Rieber
Cover design by Kathy Campbell

Contents

Introduction

B ooks have always been a significant part of my life. There just isn't any substitute for a great book. Like me, there are many people who love to read. There are also people who never developed a taste for reading, so they avoid the written word as much as possible. I believe that many people who don't enjoy reading, didn't have the opportunity to meet a book they really loved as a young person. As young children, many people are often only offered mundane, maybe satisfactory, but not the well-written stories that capture the reader's interest.

In an effort to help parents, teachers and children I've compiled this annotated list to assist in selecting books that go beyond common, boring or simply factual. I've been collecting the most interestingly written books I could locate for many years and as I sat down with each book entered in this list, I felt as though I was visiting an old friend. I found it easy to become involved in the book and difficult to put down. The goal was to do some rereading and then describe it—not as simple as it sounds when I caught myself spending hours or days enjoying the book again.

For practicality's sake I attempted to limit the amount of entries so as not to produce an overwhelming or nearly unusable book. Many parents find that their own educational background did not include much in the way of literature. Keeping that in mind I strove to provide a list of books that I knew well and could recommend—I chose not to include any negative reviews. I also excluded many of my favorite books because I eliminated purely adult books, parenting books,

books that are great additions to home libraries but could not really be classified as aiding childhood education.

Often, an entry is meant to represent many other books by the same author. Obviously, if you read a book and like it, you probably will seek out more of that writer's work. Also, if you find a certain book was not entered it does not mean it is an inferior book or did not meet my criteria. It may indicate that it was so commonly known by parents that the chances of overlooking it were near to impossible—or it may have been represented by a similar book covering virtually the same topic.

On the other hand, I made every attempt to not skimp on the children's classic literature entries even though many have been well-known mainstays for generations. You may find titles mentioned that you already own, in fact view as very obvious, those are included for the many parents whose own educational process did not afford them the opportunity to actually read classic literature and through no fault of their own are not familiar with even the most well-known titles. If you come across the opposite situation, a dearly loved book that you would have liked to see included, be sure to inform *Champion Press Ltd.* by sending a postcard to 13023 NE Hwy 99 # 7, Suite 207, Vancouver WA 98686. As I create updates of this book in the future, I will review these postcards.

In attempting to choose books for the list I kept to certain criteria. Mostly I thought of the term "a well-read person." The books had to be interesting so most of them follow the narrative style of writing. In other words, one person telling another about what they know. The books had to help in developing the love for reading and knowledge itself. My goal was to provide an easy to use format for you and a real education through real books for your students and children.

You'll find each entry has information to aid in locating the book such as an ISBN or a publisher and copyright date. Because I want you to succeed in finding the books that you want, please note these details before you begin your search for any of the books. There are many ways to locate difficult to find books. On-line searches and interlibrary loans are almost always successful. If you do meet with disappointment don't be discouraged, simply make some other selections and work with those books while your searches continue on the more elusive ones. Web sites like Amazon.Com offer out-of-print search services that can be useful as well.

You'll find a IRL for each entry as well. That stands for Independent Reading Level—these were chosen with many issues in mind. In addition to the actual, estimated reading ability, the length of the book was considered, the font size and the audience that it would probably benefit the greatest. Sometimes the IRL will have a cut off age of 8th grade for example. Obviously someone older than that would have the reading ability to read the book but if there is a cut off age suggested it means that will probably not interest the older reader as much. I would not suggest disregarding the page count provided for each book as this may impact your decision to pursue a title (or not) and at what point to introduce it to certain children. The IRL's are an indication of independent reading level only. They do not represent the interest level of the content when reading aloud to children.

The book descriptions themselves were designed to give information that will quickly help you to ascertain the value of the book for your needs and often provide information that may not be commonly known about the author, her significance, or the situation that brought about the creation of the book.

Finally, this book is designed to stand alone or as a follow-up to my first two books. In *A Charlotte Mason Education* and *More Charlotte Mason Education* I attempted to give straight forward, practicable information on "how" to teach children. Here I'm providing an answer to "what" books to use in your teaching. I strongly believe a literary education is a worthwhile and attainable goal for our children and I believe it is within reach for all of us.

Literature

A Little Princess
Frances Hodgson Burnett, Illustrated by Ethel Franklin Betts
ISBN 0-517-01480-7 (1990 edition), Children's Classics, dist. by Random House, New Jersey. HB, 272 pgs. (Printed under several publishers since 1905.)

A priceless classic that our family enjoyed reading aloud together. Burnett who was herself left penniless at the age of five writes a riches-to-rags and back again story that closely mimics her own life. This is a fabulous and memorable story that countless children have treasured.

IRL: 6th & above

A Tale of Two Cities
Charles Dickens
ISBN 0-681-41001-9 (1859), Longmeadow Press, Connecticut. HB, 448 pgs.

"It was the best of times, it was the worst of times," has stood the test of time as one of the most remembered and oft quoted opening lines in all of literature. If you're unfamiliar, the book is a historical novel dealing with Paris and London during the French Revolution. In his preface Dickens mentions Mr. Carlyle's "wonderful book" written about the same topic. I'm convinced that he is referring to Thomas Carlyle whose book has its own write-up in the history section. Reading *A Tale of Two Cities* would be a great conclusion to any study of French history.

IRL: 9th grade & above

A Very Little Child's Book of Stories
Ada M. Skinner and Eleanor L. Skinner, Illustrated by Jessie Willcox Smith
ISBN 0-517-69332-1 (1990 edition), Children's Classics, dist. by Random House, New Jersey. HB, 227 pgs. (Pub. by Dodd, Mead & Co., Inc., in 1923.)

This collection of children's favorites features the works of over fifteen authors and has eight color illustrations by Jessie Willcox Smith. The stories are grouped into three categories, The Little Child Out of Doors, In the Nursery with Mother Goose and Grandmother's Fireside Tales.

IRL: 4th to 5th grade

Aesop's Fables
Aesop, Illustrated by Nora Fry
ISBN 0-517-67901-9 (1989 edition), Children's Classics, dist. by Random House, New Jersey. HB, 203 pgs. (Originally compiled around 300 BC.)

Some doubt whether there really was an Aesop or not. He was mentioned by Plutarch, Socrates and Herodotus and the majority of people believe he did indeed live from 620 to 560 BC. Born a slave who was later freed he was killed by an angry and dishonest mob. The fables primarily use animals as main characters. Young children love to have these cute, short stories read to them. My copy has a moral attached to each fable, most of which have remained quite famous.

IRL: 4th to 5th grade

Alice's Adventures in Wonderland
Lewis Carroll, Illustrated by Bessie Pease Gutmann
ISBN 0-517-65961-1 (1988 edition), Children's Classics, dist. by Random House, New Jersey. HB, 249 pgs. (Printed under several publishers since 1865.)

Ordinarily we would not link a mathematician and fantasy author together, but that's exactly who Charles Lutwidge Dodgson (Lewis Carroll) was. He was fond of a little girl named Alice and created these adventures for her and her sisters which he verbally presented to them. The results are two of the most famous books known around the world. Fun to read silently and also a good book to share aloud—childhood just wouldn't be complete without time spent in Alice's Wonderland. IRL: 5th & above

Anne of Avonlea
Lucy Maud Montgomery, Illustrated by Stan Hunter
ISBN 0-517-08127-X (1992 edition), Children's Classics, dist. by Random House, New Jersey. HB, 204 pgs. (Originally pub. 1908.)

With this sequel to *Anne of Green Gables* the author (also an orphan) places Anne in the role of a sixteen year old school teacher. As a teacher herself, Montgomery is probably sharing from her experiences in front of a classroom. As Anne fantasizes about being a teacher she can picture a future Canadian premier "bowing low over her wrinkled hand and assuring her that it was she who had first kindled his ambition."

IRL: 8th & above

Anne of Green Gables
Lucy Maud Montgomery, Illustrated by Troy Howell
ISBN 0-517-65958-1 (1988 edition), Children's Classics, dist. by Random House, New Jersey. HB, 240 pgs. (Originally pub. 1908.)

Another extremely touching book written about an orphan, a popular topic with authors. This is Montgomery's first book and it is full of conversations—my favorite element in fiction. Anne is an unforgettable character (who would have preferred the name Cordelia) and from the beginning of the story faces many obstacles such as being sent to her new family who was expecting a boy. She also finds herself and her dramatic personality thrown in with the distant and reserved Marilla.

IRL: 6th & above

At the Back of the North Wind
George MacDonald, Illustrated by Jessie Willcox Smith
ISBN 0-517-69120-5 (1990 edition), Children's Classics, dist. by Random House, New Jersey. HB, 342 pgs. (Originally pub. in book form in 1871.)

Scottish author George MacDonald wrote on many topics before he turned his attention to creating fairy tales for his eleven children. He claimed not to write for children "but for the childlike." This book was originally written installment style for a children's magazine and ran for two years. The descriptions of Diamond's life as a boy in London have been compared to

Dickens but the encounters with the North Wind have been likened to a glorious, imaginative afterlife and to fictional places such as Oz.

IRL: 6th & above

Barchester Towers
Anthony Trollope
ISBN 0-679-40587-9 (1992 edition), Everyman's Library (Knopf), New York. HB, 277 pgs. (Printed under several publishers since 1857.)

Barchester Towers in actually a sequel to Trollope's *The Warden*, but there is vast agreement that this book stands alone and can (some even say should) be read first. It was his fifth novel, but it's the second from the Barchester set of six. This was a very disciplined author who had talent. He worked for the post office in Ireland, although he was English, and traveled by train for hours a day as part of his job. He met his self-imposed quota of 10,000 words per week writing with pencil and putting his time to good use.

IRL: 10th & above

Black Beauty
Anna Sewell
ISBN 0-517-61884-2 (1986 edition), Children's Classics, dist. by Random House, New Jersey. HB, 226 pgs. (Printed under several publishers since 1877.)

This much loved beautifully written classic is well known for its message of proper treatment of animals. It also contains valuable morals for human behavior such as strong work ethics and the abuse of alcohol. Appropriate for all age levels, you'll find that it teaches horsemanship and nineteenth century English lifestyle for a nice combination of science and history.

IRL: 5th & above

Bleak House
Charles Dickens
ISBN 0-679-40568-2 (1991 edition), Everyman's Library (Knopf) New York. HB, 880 pgs. (Printed under several publishers since 1853.)

Charles Dickens is without a doubt one the world's most talented authors and when he wrote this, as with most of his work, he did not release a skimpy book. He had the amazing ability to keep these large novels coming every few years. This one was released at roughly the same time as *Moby-Dick* and *Uncle Tom's Cabin* which brings up one reason I collect much of my literature in this Knopf set. The books include a chronological table of the author's life which coincide with other literary works and prominent events occurring at the time of the book's release.

IRL: 9th & above

Caine Mutany, The
Herman Wouk
(1951), Doubleday & Co., Inc, New York. HB, 498 pgs.

Wouk finished this book in 1951 and it's subtitled *A Novel of World War II*. He won the Pulitzer prize the following year. There is a fairly large disclaimer at the beginning of the book stating that the U. S. S. Caine did not really exist and no court-martial actually occurred. It goes further to say there are "errors of fact" within the book. The author did not intend to accurately depict naval situations but he did create a catchy story that I've seen used in other fictional works. Namely, the man in charge loses his grip on reality and something has to be done by the subordinates. Probably best appreciated by older and possibly male readers.

IRL: 10th & above

Call of the Wild, The
Jack London, Illustrated by Paul Bransom
ISBN 0-517-06003-5 (1991 edition), Children's Classics, dist. by Random House, New Jersey. HB, 255 pgs. (Printed under several publishers since 1903.)

Jack London (born in San Francisco) experienced the gold rush of 1897 while living in the Klondike. He wrote a great deal of novels and short stories, etc. but *The Call of the Wild* and *White Fang* (1906) were very successful for him. In this book we see the harsh, cold and savage Alaskan way of life through the eyes of Buck a dog kidnapped from "a big house in the sun-kissed Santa Clara Valley."

IRL: 7th & above

Canterbury Tales, The
Geoffrey Chaucer
ISBN 0-14-044022-4 (Fourteenth Century), Penguin Books, England/New York. PB, 504 pgs. (Printed under several publishers and editions.)

Finally, a translation of Chaucer that is readable and understandable without being "dumbed down." Professor Nevill Coghill (1899–1980) held many positions at Oxford and co-wrote the play version of *Canterbury Tales* which ran in London from 1968 to 1973. If you thought Chaucer was incomprehensible due to the old English I think you'll be pleasantly surprised by this translation. You do not have to be a poetry lover to enjoy this work but it would help.

IRL: 10th grade & above

Carlyle's Essay on Burns
Thomas Carlyle
(1896), American Book Co., New York. HB, 128 pgs.

As the title implies this is an essay on the life and work of poet and song writer Robert Burns (1759 to 1796). Students usually learn how to write an essay before high school graduation and one of the best preparations for that is to study other works written in this style. Much of Burns' work is recorded here including the lyrics to *Auld Lang Syne* in its original version. This book was recommended by Charlotte Mason.

IRL: 10th grade & above

Children's Stories From Dickens
Mary Angela Dickens, Illustrated by Harold Copping
ISBN 0-517-08485-6 (1993), Random House, New Jersey. HB, 119 pgs.

Usually I would only recommend reading unabridged classics as actually written by the gifted authors who wrote them. I make an exception with this book because there are many occasions to read to children who are visiting or when the need arises to buy a gift for a child who has a low likelihood to be exposed to quality literature. Plus, this is a beautifully illustrated book where ten characters have been extracted from Charles Dicken's books by his granddaughter. Chances are any child who is introduced to this book will want to read the whole book from which the story was taken. IRL: 5th & above

Complete Mother Goose, The
Unknown, Illustrated by Ethel Franklin Betts
ISBN 0-517-63383-3 (1987 edition), Children's Classics, dist. by Random House, New Jersey. HB, 227 pgs. (Printed under several publishers since the 17th and 18th Centuries.)

Some might consider this one big book of nonsense—oh well, they don't have to come over when you read it aloud. When I was a young reader I could not get enough of *The House that Jack Built* and yet I grew a little older and managed to expand my literary taste. I believe it's far more important to awaken a child to a love of books starting at the nursery level than to toss aside old favorites as being somehow beneath the modern generation. I loved reading this book aloud to my kids over and over again and the good news is my grandchildren are my next excuse to read it some more.

IRL: 3rd to 4th grade

Complete Tales of Beatrix Potter, The
Beatrix Potter
ISBN 0-7232-3618-6 (1989 edition), Penguin Group, London England. HB, 383 pgs. (Printed under several publishers since 1901 to 1930.)

Everyone is probably well acquainted with Beatrix Potter's characters and story lines. Her work is the epitome of great writing for the young audience with its broad vocabulary combined with easy to follow and entertaining stories. It's unfortunate how many of today's children are *only* exposed to poorly written, dumbed-down books. It's also a mistake to avoid children's literature completely. If you want children to love reading, love books and have a good time yourself read Beatrix Potter to them again and again.

IRL: 4th to 6th grade

Custom of the Country, The
Edith Wharton
ISBN 0-679-42301-X (1994 edition), Everyman's Library (Knopf), New York. HB, 413 pgs. (Printed under several publishers since 1913.)

Wharton, a native New Yorker, won the Pulitzer prize for *The Age of Innocence* seven years after writing this book. Her writing style reflects a marked change from 19th century to the 20th. In fact, the style reminds me of *The Great Gatsby*. Also, the topics are more modern as there are automobiles and divorces. Evidently, the custom mentioned in the title is that of American wives being looked down upon by their husbands and how that contrasted with a more feminist attitude toward marriage in Europe. The author had been living in Paris for six years when she authored this book.

IRL: 10th & above

David Copperfield
Charles Dickens
ISBN 0-679-40571-2 (1991 edition), Everyman's Library (Knopf), New York. HB, 891 pgs. (Printed under several publishers since 1850.)

Have you ever been asked this question? If you knew you were going to be stranded on a desert island and could only take three books, which three would you take? This novel would make my list. I laughed out loud and I was moved to tears as the young hero experiences death and hardships, amazing characters and survives everything thrown his way. The story is so good it would be a suitable read aloud but the length would probably prohibit its being chosen by most families. I would also be careful not force it on anyone too young to appreciate it fully.

IRL: 9th & above

Doctor Zhivago
Boris Pasternak
ISBN 0-679-40759-6 (1991 edition), Everyman's Library (Knopf), New York. HB, 510 pgs. (Printed under several publishers since 1957.)

Pasternak's most famous book was not published in Russia because of its negative view of Communism. He was coerced to by the government to decline the Nobel prize for literature in 1958. He had artistic roots with a musician for a mother and an artist for a father—his dad illustrated Tolstoy's novels. Prose-poetry is one of my favorite writing styles and it's uncommon enough but it's unheard of in a strongly political book like this one. This is a very long book and if you choose to read it realize it will be a commitment.

IRL: 12th & above

Emerson's Essays
Ralph Waldo Emerson
(1844), Educational Publishing Co., USA. HB, 185 pgs. (Some of the material was first pub. in 1835.)

Emerson, who was born in Boston in 1803, spent time in Europe where he became friends with Thomas Carlyle. He taught school, lectured, wrote poetry and (obviously) essays. The main topic in this collection is nature and originally "it took twelve years to sell five hundred copies." However, *World Book Encyclopedia* notes that his essays influenced authors such as Frost, Thoreau and Whitman and that he "has been described as belonging to the tradition of 'wisdom literature' with Confucius, Marcus Aurelius, Montaigne and Frances Bacon." (Vol. 6, 1976) This book also contains an essay on friendship and an address given at Cambridge in 1837.

IRL: 9th grade and above

Emma
Jane Austen
ISBN 0-679-40581-X (1991 edition), Alfred A Knopf, Inc., New York. HB, 459 pgs. (Printed under several publishers since 1815.)

You'll find the words, "The most perfect of Jane Austen's perfect novels" on the title page of this edition of *Emma*. Practice does make perfect and this is one of Austen's last works before her death in 1817. I love all of her novels and I don't know which I consider to be the most perfect. Her style is to include a lot of conversation all conducted with the best manners possible and to have her characters interact within an 18th century English setting. However, this novel has far less talk and more descriptions than her others. Don't push any of her work too early with children.

IRL: 9th grade & above

English Literature; for Boys and Girls
H. E. Marshall, illustrated by John R. Skelton
(1909), T. C. & E. C. Jack, Ltd., London. HB, 687 pgs.

In this work Marshall uses his rare gift to teach children the history of literature with his simple story-like style. His imaginative touch makes all the difference with this massive accomplishment. Starting with an explanation of how mankind passed down stories before writing came about and continuing through to Keats, Carlyle, Thackeray, Dickens and Tennyson. Each of the 85 chapters serves as a background before actually reading the literature itself and contains biographical information about the authors lives. A suggested reading list is offered at the close of each chapter and the hundreds of authors noticed in this work are listed chronologically.

IRL: 7th grade and above

Esterhazy
Irene Dische & Hans Magnus Enzensberger, Illustrated by Michael Sowa
ISBN 1-56846-091-0 (1993), Creative Editions, Minnesota.. HB, 30 pgs.

The Esterhazy's are a rabbit family originally from London who move to Austria and later to Berlin, in fact this book is translated from German to English. The story is good and the illustrations are of the best in quality and amusement. (My favorite is Esterhazy trying on human boxer shorts before a huge mirror.) One event portrayed is the removal of the Berlin Wall and how it effects the rabbit population. I can't recommend this book highly enough and it is worth searching for—it will become a frequent read aloud with your children.

IRL: 4th to 6th grade

George Eliot Selected Works
George Eliot
ISBN 0-517-12223-5 (1994 edition), Gramercy Books, New York. HB, 820 pgs.
(Printed under several publishers since 1861.)

Gramery prints at least thirteen different authors in these handy combined editions. You'll find the Henry James volume listed below as it is also from this set. This book contains *Silas Marner, The Lifted Veil, Brother Jacob and*

Middlemarch. George Eliot was really an English woman named Mary Ann Evans who was born in 1819. It was not uncommon to use a male pen name at that time but Evans had other reasons to obscure her identity—she had renounced her faith and lived with a man she was not married to. If you are only going to read one of her books make it *Silas Marner.*

IRL: 8th & above

Great Dog Stories
Albert Payson Terhune, Illustrated by Marguerite Kirmse
ISBN 0-517-09338-5 (1993 edition), Children's Classics, dist. by Random House, New Jersey. HB, 207 pgs. (Printed under several publishers since 1919 - 1928)

This collection was previously offered as *The Heart of a Dog* and *My Friend the Dog.* This book is written by a dog lover, particularly Collies, and is probably best appreciated by animal lovers. You'll find Lad and Lassie taking center stage in Terhune's stories. If you've been looking for some good, clean, fun reading and you happen to be a dog fanatic then you've found your book.

IRL: 6th grade & above

Heidi
Johanna Spyri, Illustrated by Jessie Willcox Smith
ISBN 0-517-61814-1 (1986 edition), Children's Classics, dist. by Crown Pub., New York. HB, 349 pgs. (Printed under several publishers since 1881.)

As with most classics *Heidi* is a highly recognizable book that endures generation to generation. Spyri lived in the Swiss Alps and as any of us who live near a mountain range know it will make a constant impression on your daily life. The majesty of nature combined with the character Heidi (another lovable orphan) makes for a great family book that can be enjoyed silently, or even better, read aloud.

IRL: 6th grade & above

Henry James Selected Works
Henry James
ISBN 0-517-11903-X (1994 edition), Gramercy Books, New York. HB, 655 pgs. (Printed under several publishers since 1881 to 1888.)

This James' Works contains *Daisy Miller: A Study, The Portrait of a Lady, The Aspern Papers, The Turn of the Screw.* James was an American, born in 1843, who allowed himself to be greatly influenced by the European writing style. He wrote over twenty novels, the most popular being *The Portrait of a Lady* and his most famous short story, *The Turn of the Screw* both included in this book.

IRL: 10th & above

House at Pooh Corner, The
A. A. Milne, Illustrated by Ernest H. Shepard
ISBN 0-525-44444-0 (1928), Dutton Children's Books, New York. HB,180 pgs.

Children's literature varies in its value and entertainment level. Parents and children have loved Milne's Pooh stories since the 1926 introduction of *Winnie-the-Pooh.* This is his sequel released two years later. The author was English, a Cambridge graduate who also wrote plays, poetry and a novel. He had written a couple of children's books when he decided to write about his son's stuffed animal collection. Many generations have benefited from that decision.

IRL: 4th to 6th grade

House of the Seven Gables, The
Nathaniel Hawthorne
ISBN 0-681-00687-0 (1851), Longmeadow Press, Connecticut. HB, 236 pgs.

Hawthorne was an American born in Salem Mass. in 1804 which may account for the witchcraft references in his two most famous books. More importantly, he was also the direct descendant of Salem judges who presided over the witchcraft trials. He has a very intelligent writing style and my advice is to realize ahead of time that you need to persevere during the early chapters in order to get to the heart of his book where the story will unfold. Incidentally, gables are any point on a roof that come together to form an angle so a rectangular house often has one gable. This edition also contains *The Scarlet Letter* and *Twice Told Tales*.

IRL: 10th grade & above

In Grandma's Attic
Arleta Richardson
ISBN 0-912692-32-4 (1974), Chariot Books, Illinois. PB, 110 pgs. (Previously pub. by several publishers.)

This book is one of ten in a series published by Chariot Books. The stories are short and pertain to a simpler time when Grandma attended classes in a one room school house. She was reared in a religious family that enjoyed wading, berry picking and swinging in the tree swing. This book is probably best suited to ten to eleven year old girls for independent reading.

IRL: 5th & 6th grade

Jane Eyre
Charlotte Brontë
ISBN 0-681-410000-0 (1990 edition), Longmeadow Press, Connecticut. HB, 457 pgs. (Printed under several publishers since 1847.)

This most famous work of the Brontë sisters is considered to be based on Charlotte's life in England. The harsh Mr. Rochester is reported to be completely fictional. The obedient yet strong-willed Jane and he *are* the book. It would benefit any reader to study a portrait of Charlotte before reading her work as I think it reveals much about her female characters. This particular edition also has Emily Brontë's *Wuthering Heights* included and an explanation of the three sisters' pen names, Charlotte's being Currer Bell, an obvious attempt to obscure her sexual identity.

IRL: 9th grade & above

Jungle Book, The
Rudyard Kipling, Illustrated by Maurice & Edward Detmold
ISBN 0-517-67902-7 (1989 edition), Children's Classics, dist. by Random House, New Jersey. HB, 303 pgs. (Printed under several publishers since 1894 & 1895.)

Believe it or not I've never seen any of the movie versions of this book—my children sure have and they love to laugh at my mispronunciations of the animal character's names. Kipling lived in India until he was five years old. When he was seventeen he turned down university money offered by his parents to return to India and write for a newspaper. Kipling was not always politically correct in his writing therefore some of his works are banned in certain school districts. *The Jungle Book* is another great read aloud book and it is possible to omit any offensive words or concepts as you are reading from it.

IRL: 6th grade & above

Kidnapped
Robert Louis Stevenson, Illustrated by N. C. Wyeth
ISBN 0-517-68783-6 (1989 edition), Children's Classics, dist. by Random House, New Jersey. HB, 241 pgs. (Printed under several publishers since 1886.)

The author based this on a true story of a murder committed in 1745. Interestingly, the hero David Balfour, I couldn't help but notice, was given Robert's second middle name—he was born Robert Lewis Balfour Stevenson. (Apparently he even took exception to the spelling of the middle name he did retain.) This novel is written in the first person and draws the reader in immediately.

IRL: 7th grade & above

Lancelot: The Adventures of King Arthur's Most Celebrated Knight
Christine Chaundler, Illustrated by Brickdale & MacKenzie
ISBN 0-517-14636-3 (1995 edition), Children's Classics, dist. by Random House, New Jersey. HB, 206 pgs. (Portions were originally pub. in Arthur and His Knights.)

Most agree that King Arthur and Lancelot probably existed. Arthur has been mentioned in various poems, etc., since the 600 and 700's AD. Personally, I chose this work over other works on King Arthur because Merlin is mentioned but not emphasized as much as in other books. In fact, Merlin dies (or sleeps "beneath the enchanted stone" after living "a long and weary life.") on page 42. The rest of story centers on Lancelot, Sir Galahad, Queen Guinevere and the Holy Grail.

IRL: 7th grade & above

Legend of Pocahontas, The
Virginia Watson, Illustrated by George Wharton Edwards
ISBN 0-517-12225-1 (1995 edition), Children's Classics, dist. by Random House, New Jersey. HB, 208 pgs. (Printed under several publishers since the 1900's.)

Pocahontas was a real person but as is the case with many legendary people no one can be certain that all the stories written about her are completely true. She did indeed marry John Rolfe in 1614 and traveled with him to London in 1616. Regardless of any potential embellishments this is a memorable story of Native American culture and the impact White settlers had when landing on the new continent. Children love this book and it was a another great read aloud for us.

IRL: 7th grade & above

Little Men
Louisa May Alcott, Illustrated by Troy Howell
ISBN 0-517-03088-8 (1991 edition), Children's Classics, dist. by Random House Co., New York. HB, 202 pgs. (Printed under several publishers since 1871.)

This book picks up where *Little Women* ended and its emphasis on boys rather than girls gives readers a chance to expose their children to Alcott regardless of their sex. Jo and her husband Professor Bhaer have opened a school which is already running when Nat, the new boy, arrives with a letter from Teddy also known as Mr. Lawrence a key character from the previous book. As art so frequently imitates life, Plumfield the school, is patterned after Alcott's father's New England schools.

IRL: 6th grade & above

Little Women
Louisa May Alcott, Illustrated by Jessie Willcox Smith
ISBN 0-517-63489-9 (1987 edition), Children's Classics, dist. by Random House Co., New Jersey. HB, 388 pgs. (Printed under several publishers since 1869.)

There is a consensus that the March family and the Alcott family were one and the same with Jo playing the part of Louisa who was also the second in the birth order among her three sisters. For me it was both fortunate and unfortunate that I did not read *Little Women* until I was in my thirties. That made reading the book for the first time a real treat and I enjoyed every minute of it but it's also a reflection of the poor literary choices made by the educational system during my generation. Alcott is a gifted author who truly gave us a "must read" book when she wrote this.

IRL: 7th grade & above

Load of Unicorn, The
Cynthia Harnett
ISBN 0-1403-0257-3 (1959), Penguin Books Ltd., England. PB, 249 pgs.

Harnett, an award winning author, wrote this in modern English that's easy to understand but it's set in the 1400's. The story has nothing to do with Unicorns, the fictitious animal, instead it happens to be the name of a certain printing paper available at the time. Bendy, the main character works with his family as a scribe. They copy books by hand for a living because the printing press had not yet been invented. As the typeset books begin to make their appearance Bendy has to choose between the old way which means siding with his family or switching to the competitor's side.

IRL: 6th to 9th grade

Moby Dick
Herman Melville
ISBN 0-679-40559-3 (1991 edition), Everyman's Library (Knopf), New York. HB, 592 pgs. (Printed under several publishers since 1851.)

Melville inscribed this book to Nathaniel Hawthorne "In token of my admiration for his genius." It a good thing he gave Hawthorne this compliment as it turns out he had everything to do with Melville's success with *Moby Dick*. This was the author's sixth book and he had written it travel-journal style as with some of his previous works. He had been on the sea a great deal and had worked on a whaling ship. At the last possible chance he met Hawthorne who convinced him to convert it into fiction and release it as a novel. Many children have made the unfortunate choice to avoid literature because this book was forced on them. Learn from other's mistakes and let this be a voluntary book.

IRL: 10th & above

Old Curiosity Shop, The
Charles Dickens
ISBN 0-679-44373-8 (1995 edition), Everyman's Library (Knopf), New York. HB, 569 pgs. (Printed under several publishers since 1840.)

In Dickens' chronology this work follows *Oliver Twist* and preceeds *A Christmas Carol* and *David Copperfield*. It was written as a serial and released on a weekly basis. Dickens usually didn't have a plot firmly mapped out in his mind when he began his novels, but he claimed after its completion that this story was plotted. He also knew he wanted to "surround the lonely figure of the child with grotesque and wild, but not impossible, companions." He certainly accomplished this goal in the character of Quilp, possibly the most grotesque fictional personality ever created.

IRL: 8th & above

Our Village
Mary Russell Mitford, Illustrated by Hugh Thomson
(1902), MacMillan and Co., Ltd., New York. HB, 256 pgs.

This book is very different in writing style. For example it is completely void of conversations which makes it as unlike a Jane Austen novel as possible. Mainly, Mitford is describing her fellow villagers and the various plant life in vivid detail. In all honesty the fifty page introduction about Mitford herself was my favorite part. She was born in 1787, loved her books, flowers and friends and on her tenth birthday choose the winning lottery numbers resulting in a prize of 20,000 pounds which restored her family to its original affluence.

IRL: 6th grade & above

Oliver Twist
Charles Dickens
ISBN 0-681-41001-9 (1839), Longmeadow Press, Connecticut. HB, 509 pgs.

In Dicken's preface to this book he declared that the depictions of criminals up to that point in current literature had not been realistic and decided to "paint them in all their deformity, in all their wretchedness, in all the squalid misery of their lives, to show them as they really were." To choose this work as a family read-aloud will take true commitment, however, it serves as one of my primary examples of good literature with high vocabulary and a story line that even the youngest child will understand. This edition also contains *A Tale of Two Cities.*

IRL: 8th grade & above

Persuasion
Jane Austen

ISBN 0-679-40986-6 (1992 edition), Alfred A Knopf, Inc., New York. HB, 260 pgs. (Printed under several publishers since 1816.)

Jane Austen could have never known how enduring and well respected her work would be and how many movies would later come from her books. (Incidentally, my advice is always read a book before seeing the movie.) Anne, the main character of this book is a bit different from Austen's usual lead female. She's likable, of course, but she's the victim of persuasion resulting in a lack of fulfillment and resignation in her life. Some critics have even referred to Anne as melancholy but as a Jane Austen fan you'll not get any critical remarks from me on her work or characters.

IRL: 9th grade & above

Pollyanna
Eleanor H. Porter, Illustrated by Terry Hoff
ISBN 0-517-11987-0 (1994 edition), Children's Classics, dist. by Random House Co., New Jersey. HB, 204 pgs. (Printed under several publishers since 1913.)

Aunt Polly is asked to take in eleven-year-old Pollyanna which she considers to be a "disagreeable" duty she must perform for the orphaned child of her sister. Instead of giving her a regular bedroom she has the help clean out one of the attics. Attics, cranky aunts or paralysis cannot keep Pollyanna from seeing the bright side of everything.

IRL: 6th grade & above

Portrait of a Lady, The
Henry James
ISBN 0-679-40562-3 (1991 edition), Alfred A Knopf, Inc., New York. HB, 626 pgs. (Printed under several publishers since 1881.)

I really enjoyed this book and recently sat down with my children to watch a video version of it. This movie had a well-known cast and as I was very eager to have my family's full attention I was going on and on about the greatness of the book and how much they were going to love it. The previews had convinced me that the wardrobe and sets were going to be accurate. After getting through the slightly odd opening credits we soon came to the first perverted scene which convinced my kids that they really didn't know their mother. I insisted that the book was nothing like that and it wasn't. It's great literature with an intriguing story.

IRL: 11th grade & above

Pride and Prejudice
Jane Austen
ISBN 0-679-40542-9 (1991 edition), Alfred A Knopf, Inc., New York. HB, 368 pgs. (Printed under several publishers since 1813.)

This was the first Austen book I read and the conversations, descriptions and characters both hooked and impressed me. Having good manners and possessing the traits of a good conversationalist was the first thing any new man in town was judged on. Whether one was well read or not was the next deciding factor for popularity in Jane's novels. Elizabeth, the heroine in this book has been the most closely associated character with the author much like Jo in Alcott's *Little Women*.

IRL: 9th grade & above

Prince and the Pauper, The
Mark Twain, Illustrated by William Cathedral
ISBN 0-517-11815-7 (1994 edition), Children's Classics, dist. by Random House Co., New Jersey. HB, 294 pgs. (Printed under several publishers since 1882.)

American born Samuel Clemens set this novel in 16th Century England in which the son of King Henry the VIII changes clothes and identities with a look alike stranger born into poverty. Both Twain and I think that this is one of his very best writings—it is beautifully authored, but many literary critics disagree. There are quite a few "writhe" and "methinks" in the conversations, if you're good at English accents and you love to see "eth" at the end of a word then go for the read aloud.

IRL: 7th grade & above

Quite Early One Morning
Dylan Thomas
(1954), New Directions, New York. HB, 240 pgs.

This is the American version (not the English) collection of stories, essays and poetry written over a ten year period. The author, before his sudden and early death, had planned to release a book by this title. The English version has less entries than the American one because the selections are restricted only to those entries broadcasted verbally by Thomas. The edition named here has twenty–five pieces including my favorite, *Reminiscences of Childhood*. It also has the famous, *A Child's Christmas in Wales*.

IRL: 9th & above

Rebecca of Sunny brook Farm
Kate Douglas Wiggins, Illustrated by Peter Fiore
ISBN 0-517-09275-1 (1993 edition), Children's Classics, dist. by Random House, New Jersey. HB, 234 pgs. (Printed under several publishers since 1903.)

Rebecca is not an orphan—she has a mother who puts her on a mail carrying stage coach so that she can live with her aunts. She is the second of seven, the last child who was born the day their father died. You'll find Rebecca is talkative and likable. I read this book to myself and liked it so much I read it aloud to all of my children.

IRL: 7th grade & above

Robin Hood
Louis Read, Illustrated by Frank Godwin

ISBN 0-517-61729-8 (1987 edition), Children's Classics, dist. by Random House, New Jersey. HB, 286 pgs. (Printed under several publishers since the early 1900's.)

Read wrote this book borrowing ideas from ballads dating as early as the 14th century that mentioned Robin Hood's name. Traditionally, Robin and his merry men lived their outlaw life in the late 1100's but mention of stealing from the rich to give to the poor was absent from the early verses. Many authors have added elements since then leaving current readers with a combination of attributes that the legendary Robin Hood probably did not have originally. This book provided our family an exceptionally great read aloud.

IRL: 8th grade & above

Robinson Crusoe
Daniel Defoe, Illustrated by N. C. Wyeth

ISBN 0-517-01757-1 (1990 edition), Children's Classics, dist. by Random House, New Jersey. HB, 287 pgs. (Printed under several publishers since 1719.)

Defoe wrote for a newspaper for about twenty–five years and ran a periodical for nine years. He came across a true story of a man stranded on uninhabited island for five years which later became his inspiration for writing *Robinson Crusoe* fairly late in his life. Written in the first person it certainly is a riveting story and considered by many a masterpiece. His other well-known novel is *Moll Flanders*.

IRL: 8th grade & above

Scarlet Letter, The
Nathaniel Hawthorne
ISBN 0-681-00687-0 (1850), Longmeadow Press, Connecticut. HB, 170 pgs.

If you were unfortunate enough to see 1995 movie version of *The Scarlet Letter* without having read the book you would not be aware of how far off that "freely adapted" version was. This is not a sexual book, it's considered a masterpiece of literature. It is written in a deep, complex manner that I feel has deliberate intentions to compel the reader to return to the book for multiple readings. It's a brief, yet important, look at Puritan judgments and morals, and it followed Hawthorne's periodical writing as his first novel.

IRL: 11th grade & above

Secret Garden, The
Frances Hodgson Burnett, Illustrated by Troy Howell
ISBN 0-517-63225-X (1987 edition), Children's Classics, dist. by Random House, New Jersey. HB, 272 pgs. (Printed under several publishers since 1912.)

A well known and endearing story with memorable characters, the concept of finding a secret garden in the midst of an otherwise bleak life captures the imagination of young and old. As with the majority of classic literature it is always best to read the book before seeing the motion picture. If you've already seen the movie, you'll enjoy seeing the characters differently than on screen.

IRL: 6th grade & above

Selections From Irving's Sketch Book
Washington Irving, Edited by Robert P. St. John
(1892), American Book Co., New York. HB, 205 pgs.

The term "sketch book" in the above title may lead one to think of drawings and illustrations. Instead these are written sketches by a observant and well-traveled author. Irving was born in 1783 in New York City and was admired by Sir Walter Scott whose praise is well-deserved as Irving has an outstanding writing style. Topics covered include an autobiography, English Christmas customs, book making, commentary on *The Legend of Sleepy*

Hollow, Rip Van Winkle and various travel experiences describing the Westminster Abbey and Stratford-On-Avon. If locating a copy of *Selections* proves to be difficult try finding the complete editions originally published by Putnam's Sons.

IRL: 9th grade & above

Sense and Sensibility
Jane Austen

ISBN 0-679-40987-4 (1992 edition), Alfred A Knopf, Inc., New York. HB, 380 pgs. (Printed under several publishers since 1812.)

In this book we have two sisters Elinor and Marianne each represented in the title. One has sense and the other is dreamy, poetic and imaginative. Her senses and emotion rule her life. They, their mother and younger sister are displaced from their large estate and forced to move to a "cottage" and live a far more humble life. Great characters, (this one has the immoral Willoughby) great story and great writing make this one of Austen's best.

IRL: 9th grade & above

Shakespeare
William Shakespeare

ISBN 1-85152-492-4 (1995), Chancellor Press, Great Britain. PB, 500 pgs.

ISBN 0-14-015008-01 (1997), Penguin Books, USA. PB, 792 pgs.

ISBN 0-679-41741-9 (1992), Everyman's Library (Knopf), New York. HB, 248 pgs.

ISBN 0-681-41003-5, Longmeadow Press, USA. HB, 1240 pgs.

That any Shakespearean work is worth mentioning as a literary classic goes without saying and no one will have any trouble locating his books. The above mentioned ISBN's are each listed for different reasons. The first is an inexpensive, yet durable paperback containing *Hamlet, Macbeth, King Lear* and *Othello*. Also, for paperbacks, this set has beautiful art work on the covers and the words do not run into the spine. The second is also an inexpensive paperback called *The Portable Shakespeare*. It has seven of the plays and is very readable and very well bound. My suggestion is to collect several copies in the less costly versions so that your family members can all read the same play together. The third is from a set beautifully bound in gray cloth—this one contains *The Sonnets and Narrative Poems*. These are great to collect or give as gifts. The last one listed above is called *The Complete Works of William Shakespeare* and is larger than a lot of Bibles. It contains everything and has a dividing line in the center of each page with fairly small print. This is a very fine copy with gilt pages and every home should probably invest in one of the complete works in order to have all of his writing on hand.

IRL: 9th grade & above

Swiss Family Robinson, The
Johann Wyss, Illustrated by Robinson & Winter
ISBN 0-517-06022-1 (1993 edition), Children's Classics, dist. by Random House, New Jersey. HB, 274 pgs. (Printed under several publishers since 1813.)

This book was truly a family affair from its conception to its publication. Evidently they were fans of the book *Robinson Crusoe* as many have noted the similarities and they liked to spend time pretending they had been shipwrecked. This led to telling stories to one another which the father, Johann, wrote. One of his sons illustrated and the other took responsibility to edit and publish it. The fact that Wyss was a clergyman comes through in his book about a family of six, abandoned by the crew of the ship and forced to survive by their wits and cooperation with each other.

IRL: 8th grade & above

Tales From Shakespeare
Charles & Mary Lamb, Illustrated by Shippen & Elliot
ISBN 0-517-62156-8 (1986 edition), Children's Classics, dist. by Random House, New Jersey. HB, 377 pgs. (Printed under several publishers since 1807.)

This brother and sister collaborated in paraphrasing twenty of Shakespeare's works. He authored the tragedies and Mary the comedies. Charles and Mary resided together until his death in 1834. Charles had an aversion for what he called "namby-pamby" also known as twaddle and now commonly referred to as "dumbed down." They succeeded in converting these complicated works into prose without sacrificing the vocabulary or the beauty and produced something easier to understand with above average literary quality. IRL: 8th grade & above

Twice Told Tales
Nathaniel Hawthorne
ISBN 0-681-00687-0 (1850), Longmeadow Press, Connecticut. HB, 339pgs.

Hawthorne wrote over 100 tales that were published in various periodicals and later collected and published as *Twice Told Tales*. Longmeadow published thirty–six in this edition. Hawthorne was an extremely gifted author and these captivating short stories consist of such imaginative plots that many, if not all of them would have made great, full length novels. They remind me of campfire stories but they are far more creative. The only unfortunate thing I have to mention is the rare use of a certain unacceptable racial slur, as always, a little editing while reading aloud will eradicate the problem.

IRL: 11th grade & above

Treasure Island
Robert Louis Stevenson, Illustrated by Milo Winter
ISBN 0-517-61816-8 (1986 edition), Children's Classics, dist. by Random House, New Jersey. HB, 258 pgs. (Printed under several publishers since 1883.)

This is Stevenson's first and considered to be his most well-known novel. Sickly as he was, he lived all over the world and had an affinity to sea travel. Our family started this book as a read aloud but having no talent whatsoever for accents, especially pirate jargon, I chose to abandon the project. Instead I ask that my children read this one silently and enjoy all that wonderful "Ay, ay, matey" colloquialisms in the confines of their imaginations.

IRL: 7th grade & above

Treasures of the Snow
Patricia St. John
ISBN 0-8024-0008-6 (1952), The Moody Bible Institute, USA. PB, 255 pgs.

St. John, who has written at least seven other books, considers herself to be a missionary. When she was seven she moved to Switzerland where this book is set and she participated in the same lifestyle as the children in her story. This book has been popular among Christians because the bully goes through a conversion resulting in the main topics being salvation and forgiveness.

IRL: 6th grade & above

Water Babies, The
Charles Kingsley, Illustrated by Jessie Willcox Smith
ISBN 0-681-00647-1 (1994, originally pub. 1863), Longmeadow Press, Connecticut. HB, 279 pgs.

This modern edition of Kingsley's popular fantasy has slight omissions. For example, the original included excerpts from poets such as Wordsworth and Coleridge. However, this version or any other currently in-print one will be easier to locate. Plus. any fan of Jessie Willcox Smith will be delighted with her illustrations. This copy also has a child-friendly-sized font that will ease independent reading. See the following entry for more on *The Water Babies*.

IRL: 6th grade & above

Water Babies, The & Madam How and Lady Why
Charles Kingsley
(1863 Original pub.), Frank F. Lovell & Co., New York. HB, 408 pgs. (Inc. both books)

This older version of *The Water Babies* includes a copy of the hard to find *Madam How and Lady Why* (pub. 1868) which comes highly recommended by Charlotte Mason. The former is subtitled, *A Fairy Tale for a Land-Baby* and it's dedicated to the author's youngest son. Tom is a mistreated chimney sweep who is transformed into a water baby and lives among the fish and other creatures. Madam How and Lady Why are both fairies who help to differentiate between what we can know and what we can't. Topic covered are Earthquakes, Volcanoes, Soil, Ice, Chalk, Coral Reefs and Fields. This would be most useful as a read-aloud for younger children.

IRL: 7th grade & above

Where Angels Fear to Tread
E. M. Forster

ISBN 0-517-14782-3 (1993 edition), Gramercy Books, New York. HB, 503 pgs. (Printed under several publishers since 1905.)

Forster's writing style has been likened to Jane Austen's. He too was English and therefore he sets his scenes and characters in Europe. *Where Angels Fear to Tread* is an excellent story and one not to be overlooked when making literary choices. His writing style is best appreciated through silent reading and I would not recommend his work to be read aloud. This particular copy also contains *A Room with a View* and *Howard's End*.

IRL: 10th grade & above

Winnie-the-Pooh
A. A. Milne, Illustrated by Ernest H. Shepard

ISBN 0-525-44443-2 (1926), Dutton Children's Books, New York. HB,161 pgs.

Okay, this is one instance where I was introduced to the video and TV version long before the actual book. I always liked the Pooh shows I saw but I was in for a huge surprise when I finally read Milne's books to my kids. Before the books Eeyore was my least favorite character. In the written format he is the funniest by far. This is great read aloud stuff for young children and it gives the reading adult a chance to really enjoy the time.

IRL: 4th grade & above

Wuthering Heights
Emily Brontë

ISBN 0-681-410000-0 (1990 edition), Longmeadow Press, Connecticut. HB, 306 pgs. (Printed under several publishers since 1847.)

This is Emily's only novel. When her sister Charlotte discovered her unpublished poetry she found, "it took hours to reconcile her [the person] to the discovery . . . and days to persuade her that such poems merited publication." Emily's pen name was Ellis Bell and her work was accepted by a publisher before Charlotte's was. She was also the first of the sisters to pass away. Her poetic tendencies show through in her prose which is one of my favorite writing styles.

IRL: 10th grade & above

History

A Brief History of the United States
John Bach McMaster
(1907), American Book Co., New York. HB , 440 pgs.

Many people have told me that they are looking for a comprehensive overview of U. S. history. Although there are many of these written they do tend to be on the dry side. This particular book is one that has a "textbook" look but is actually interesting to read. Starting with the discovery of the U.S. and ending at the turn of the 20th Century, it contains copies of historical documents such as the Declaration of Independence and a handwritten excerpt from the Emancipation Proclamation.

IRL: 8th grade & above

A History of England
H. O. Arnold-Forster
Cassell & Co., Ltd., London & New York. HB , 802 pgs. (Vol 1 & 11 combined.)

This is one of the most detailed and thorough coverage of English history that I own. In fact it is so comprehensive that it may contain far more information than the average American student needs. The writing is interesting and the many charts provided feature topics like the reigns and chronological details of a monarch's life. Lists also enable the student to see at a glance the names of other famous people who lived during each King and Queen's reign. Other topics include, Poets, laws, wars, inventions, etc.

IRL: 8th grade & above

Abraham Lincoln's Don'ts
Abraham Lincoln, Selected & Arranged by Wayne Whipple
(1918), Henry Altemus Co., Philadelphia., 96 pgs.

I love this little book although I would have named it Abraham Lincoln's Do's. It consists of small quotations straight from Lincoln's mouth and really provides a glimpse into his personality and opinions. It can be read in its entirety in about one hour, however, you'll want to read it again and again. This would make for outstanding copy work for younger student due to its thoughtfulness and large font. "I will write my state papers myself, and the people will understand them. The time will never come in this country when people won't know what 'sugar-coated' means." (p. 67)

IRL: 5th grade & above

American History, A Survey
Current, Williams, Freidel & Brinkley
ISBN 0-394-33043-9 (1959-updated frequently), Alfred A. Knopf, New York. HB , 976 pgs.

This book is in every way a textbook, however, no home library is complete without a book like this one. Not only will it be a useful tool but you'll find it almost as indispensable as an encyclopedia or dictionary. A thorough coverage of history like this one can (and should) take the place of several shelved history textbooks that families keep just in case they need to look something up. This one is fairly well-written and illustrated, contains many suggested readings, has good indexes, provides the Declaration of Independence and lists the presidential elections including all candidates, their parties and votes counted back to George Washington.

IRL: 11th grade & above

American History Stories...You Never Read in School... but should have
Mara L. Pratt, M.D.
ISBN 0-9640546-0-4 (1993), The Randall Co., USA. PB ,150 pgs.

Reed Simonsen found a 1889 copy of this book at a used book sale. After he found himself staying up all night to read it he decided it was valuable enough to put back into print. He certainly made the right choice—it's easy to read and easy to love. I have read it aloud to all age levels and found its short chapters very conducive both for attention span and comprehension. Highly recommended.

IRL: 6th grade & above

American Notes
Rudyard Kipling
J. H. Sears & Co., Inc., New York. 239 pgs.

Nobel prize-winning Kipling was not always well-received or readily respected. He was thoroughly English and tended to support British colonialism (meaning the spread of the kingdom throughout the world). In this book he gives his account of crossing the Atlantic by ship in order to visit America. Eyewitness accounts are always the most valuable and this work is far more than a travel log. His descriptions are vivid whether he is writing of ocean travel, American politics or our conglomeration of immigrants all calling themselves "Americans." Bear in mind that this author did not employ politically correct terminology and an occasional word could (and should) be omitted when reading aloud.

IRL: 6th grade & above

Autobiography of Benjamin Franklin, The
Benjamin Franklin
Written between 1771 and 1789, Houghton Mifflin Co. (c. 1923), USA. HB (PB available), 235 pgs. (Printed under several publishers.)

Franklin's first words in this book are: *Dear Son*. This may explain the intimacy and frank detail in which the book is written. I found it to be one of my all-time favorite books and immediately devoured it. Much can be learned about our country and the social/economic circumstances Franklin found himself in. This book serves as a perfect example of how much history can be retained even when the material centers around one life. Enjoyable enough to be reread numerous times.

IRL: 7th grade & above

Bard of Avon: The Story of William Shakespeare
Diane Stanley & Peter Vennema, Illustrated by Diane Stanley
ISBN 0-688-09108 (1992), Morrow Junior Books, New York. HB, 48 pgs.

This book provides a friendly introduction for the younger child to Shakespeare. As an adult I learned and retained a lot from this book about the playwright and his family. Covering 1569 to 1616 with as much accuracy as possible the authors did not include any boring or unnecessary detail. Instead they wrote a great read aloud that you can reread and use as a picture book with above average illustrations. The postscript is most interesting where the famous phrases we use in everyday language such as "seen better days" or "tongue-tied" are identified as Shakespearean.

IRL: 4th to 6th grade

Bulfinch's Mythology
Thomas Bulfinch, revised by Rev. E. E. Hale
(1884), originally copyrighted 1858, S. W. Tilton & Co. Pub., New York. HB, 404 pgs.

This beautifully illustrated book starts with 169 pages on King Arthur and His Knights. The second section is called the Mabinogeon and covers the Britons, the Welsh, and then presents The Lady of the Fountain, Geraint, Pwyll, Branwen, Manawyddan, Kilwich and Olwen, Peredur and Taliesin. Part three deals with The Knights of English History including King Richard, Robin Hood, Chevy Chase and Edward the Black Prince. This is a wonderful combination of historical fact and legend and it was used in the Charlotte Mason schools.

IRL: 8th grade & above

Child's History of England
Charles Dickens
Rand, McNally & Co., New York. HB , 470 pgs.

As commonly done with English history this book begins in 50 BC. It is a very thorough and warmly written book that covers everything up to 1837 when Queen Victoria took the throne. Due to its exceeding detail I would recommend reading from it rather than through it. Or it could be assigned to an older child for independent reading and as the only English history book they would really need. Of course it is very well written and I could spend months with this book and be extremely entertained.

IRL: 8th grade & above

Christmas in the Northwest: 1791-1929
Compiled by Gary Fuller Reese
(1995), Media Production Assoc., Tacoma, WA. PB , 80 pgs. (Pub. sponsored by Historic Fort Steilacoom Assoc. WA.)

Beginning with the first celebration ever recorded in the Northwest (1791) Reese describes the feast given by Captain Gray for fifty individuals aboard the *Columbia* anchored by Vancouver Island (which had yet to named or explored by Captain Vancouver). The entire book is largely written by first-hand eye witnesses and offers over fifty accounts featuring various locations such as Whidbey Island, Fort Nisqually and Seattle. Excerpts from Lewis & Clark's diaries are included as they pertain to Christmas.

IRL: 6th grade & above

Conversations with Pioneer Women
Fred Lockley
ISBN 0-931742-0-80 (1981), Rainy Day Press, PB, 310 pgs,

This is an important, accurate and touching book. It was decided to verbally interview survivors of the Oregon Trail crossing at the turn of the 20th century before they all passed away. Some entries are extremely short and some run for pages. In the first person, these women retell the hardships, illnesses and deaths they witnessed. Many of them were orphans, the sole survivors of the family who had originally set out for the West. You and your children will know, really know, why diseases such as Cholera were truly catastrophic and how fast they killed entire families and other details of what it was really like to make that journey. Highly recommended.

IRL: 8th grade & above

England's Story
Eva March Tappan Ph. D
(1901), Houghton, Mifflin & Co., USA. HB, 370 pgs.

Tappin's book originated from talks given to high school freshmen and does indeed have the look of a textbook due to its section titles and layout. However, she succeeded in writing a friendly narrative spanning from 55 BC through the nineteenth century. Wars, reigns, poets and monarchs are interestingly presented in chronological order with special attention to historical figures the author thought students would encounter later in their studies. It served well as a read-aloud to my young students but it's also a book adult history buffs would read for pleasure.

IRL: 8th grade & above

French Revolution, The
Thomas Carlyle
(1906), J. M. Dent & Sons Ltd. London. HB, 399 pgs. (Vol. 1 & 2. Originally pub. 1837)

Carlyle who was born in Scotland in 1795 was a well-known author and lecturer. When he wrote *The French Revolution* and the only copy was accidentally burned—he chose to rewrite it. He must have had a passion for the topic as seen in this excerpt, "For the present, our *Citoyens* chant chorally *To arms*; and have no arms! Arms are searched for; passionately; there is joy over any musket. Moreover, entrenchments shall be made round Paris . . . coffins of the dead are raised; for melting into balls. All Church-bells must down into the furnace to make canon; all Church-plate into the mint to make money." (p. 138, Vol. 11)

IRL: 9th grade & above

George Washington Carver
Rackham Holt
(1943), Double Day, Doran & Co., New York. HB, 342 pgs.

This is a biography of Dr. Carver's life but it's also much more. This is a post slavery history of America in the 1800's. Emancipation did not bring about immediate change in areas such as education. Right before the U.S.

had compulsory attendance The Negro Reconstruction Government of Alabama "created a free public-school system, from which the whites benefited also." Soon after the state constitution ordered segregation in schools. This is a good biography, easy-to-read and offers an opportunity to learn a lot about an important turning point in history.

IRL: 8th & above

George Washington the Christian
William J. Johnson
(1992), Christian Liberty Press, USA. (Originally pub. 1919) PB, 299 pgs.

Johnson writes in his preface that there was no attempt made to "analyze" George Washington's religion but only by providing the evidence through magazines, books, letters, speeches, diaries and other papers he allows the reader to form his own opinion. These original sources are used abundantly, given in chronological order and stringently referenced throughout.

IRL: 8th to 11th grade

Gold Rush, The
Liza Ketchum
ISBN 0-316-49047-4 (1996), Little, Brown & Company, New York. PB , 118 pgs.

This is one of three "companion volumes" to the Public Television Series *The West*. One of my sons found it and had to have it. My guess is the numerous authentic black and white photographs caught his attention. The text is very good as well and based on true stories and real people. Life and death conditions are portrayed both in the journey out west and in daily practices in the mining camps. According to this book a typical soldier was more than willing to trade his typical income of seven dollars per month in for a potential of hundreds per day. But the gold rush attracted people from all walks of life—their stories and strife varied but their motivation for gold was universal.

IRL: 6th to 9th grade

Great Words From Great Americans
G. P. Putnam's Sons
(1889), G. P. Putnam's Sons, New York. HB , 207 pgs.

Every home should have a book like this one in order to refer to these famous words at a moment's notice. This collection contains The Declaration of Independence (1776), The Constitution of the United States (1789), Washington's and Lincoln's first and second Inaugural Speeches, plus Washington's Farewell Address and Lincoln's Gettysburg Address. It also provides other helpful entries including an index to the constitution.

IRL: 10th & above

Heroes, The
Charles Kingsley, Retold by Mary MacGregor
E. P. Dutton & Co., New York. HB, 115 pgs.

MacGregor did an exceptional job of simplifying Kingsley's work (see next entry) into something younger children can comprehend but is in no way dumbed down. She left out names of the less prominent characters, included more paragraph breaks and worked with a larger font. The final result is a book that will not scare away the younger reader. *The Heroes* covers Perseus, the Argonauts and Theseus.

IRL: 6th grade & above

Heroes or Greek Fairy Tales, The
Charles Kingsley
(1895), Henry Altemus, Philadelphia. HB, 208 pgs.

Kingsley thought that the Greek culture had left such a significant mark on the world by leaving us with mathematics, geometry, geography, astronomy, laws, freedom, politics and a great language that they could hardly be ignored. Assuming that children would cover the Greek myths during the educational process he thought an early introduction was in order. He brings his Christianity and disapproval of idol worship to the tales without interfering with the stories. This work is a good example of writing "to" children rather than "down to" them. The IRL would be set at 6th grade, however, the Greek names will present a slight difficulty for the modren child.

IRL: 8th grade & above

Hiding Place, The
Corrie ten Boom
ISBN 0-553-25669-6 (1971), Bantam Books, New York. PB, 241 pgs.

Corrie carried out her dying sister's words to go and tell people about life in Nazi concentration camps and how God had helped them during their severe persecution. This deeply religious book portrays sacrifice and forgiveness far beyond most people's capabilities. Maybe the writing isn't at masterpiece level but the content has that unique eyewitness approach to what can only be described as a holocaust.

IRL: 8th grade & above

History of England, Vol. 1, 2, 3, & 4
Lord Macaulay
(1967), Heron Books, London. HB, Four Volumes each close to or over 600 pgs.

Macaulay began this work in 1838 and followed a self-imposed quota of words per day until his death in 1859. The last passages had to be deciphered by his sister. These extensive volumes were bestsellers and are for the serious reader only. This work has an outstanding reputation because of its vast information and ease of reading.

IRL: 12th grade & above

History of Julius Caesar
Jacob Abbott
(1877), Harper & Brothers, Publishers, New York. HB, 278 pgs.

Abbott wrote a large quantity of books. He has a series designed for little children, a set of science books and thirty–four illustrated histories including this one on Julius Caesar. President Abraham Lincoln had this to say of Abbot's work, "Your Series of Histories gives me, in brief compass, just that knowledge of past men and events which I need. I have read them with the greatest interest . . . I am indebted for about all the historical knowledge I have." This book is interesting, informative and done in chronological order.

IRL: 8th grade & above

In Freedom's Cause: A Story of Wallace & Bruce
G. A. Henty
(1894), The Federal Book Co., New York. HB ,362 pgs.

In Freedom's Cause: A Story of Wallace & Bruce
G. A. Henty
ISBN 1-887159-03-7 (1997), Preston Speed Publications, Pennsylvania. HB, 337 pgs. Paperback ISBN 1-887159-35-5, Phone 909-337-7391 or email Leggewie@msn.com

Preston Speed has obtained Henty's work in its entirety which amounts to 80 to 90 books in all and they are committed to printing two new Henty's per month. At this time they have 24 of them in print. The older copy I have is extremely frail, with dark brown pages that threaten to fall apart at any reading. Henty's books have become very popular since I first discovered his work in the antique stores. While I enjoy antique books these new copies are preferable with their acid-free paper and larger font. This book covers William Wallace, Robert Bruce and the war between Scotland and England in 1314.

IRL: 7th grade & above

John Adams and the American Revolution
Catherine Drinker Bowen
(1949), Little, Brown and Company, Boston. HB, 699 pgs.

Bowen wrote that she chose the narrative writing form because "it is the most persuasive." She used easily accessible and verifiable facts that were obtained through letters, newspapers, diaries and other historic literature— her extensive bibliography speaks for itself. The work begins in 1746 and serves as a very detailed biography of Adams' life (the second president) and a reliable history of the early United States.

IRL: 8th grade & above

Key to the Prison
Louise A. Vernon
ISBN: 0-8361-1813-8 (1968), Herald Press, Pennsylvania. PB, 139 pgs.

Vernon wrote many books and her style involves re-creating stories of prominent people who have a historical place in church history. Her format uses a child placed in the center of the action, in this case, Tommy Stafford is the fictional child who witnesses the life of George Fox. This is a heavily religious book that teaches about the beginning of the Quaker church, also known as the Society of Friends. I recommend this for independent reading in late grade school.

IRL: 5th to 6th grade

Kingfisher Illustrated History of the World
Kingfisher Books
ISBN: 1-85697-862-1 (1992), Kingfisher Books, New York. HB, 761 pgs.

This is a reference book much like a one volume encyclopedia. It's probably best used as a tool to look for quick information in order to solidify a particular era after reading literary history. The format is chronological, a must for me, and has an index to save researching time. Kingfisher tried to increase the interest level with illustrations and photographs that are not overwhelming and by including information on people, arts and crafts, architecture, religion, etc. If you leave a copy in an accessible place you'll find it's also the kind of book family members will thumb through.

IRL: 6th to 8th grade

Kings and Things; First Stories from English History
H. E. Marshall
(1937), Thomas Nelson and Sons, Ltd. HB, 399 pgs.

Marshall is my favorite author in the area of history. In this book he wanted to create a bedtime story book that gave British children an outline of their history rather than constantly reading fairy tales and other children's books. He thought the topic was "neglected because it is thought to be a story too frightening or too difficult for the very young person's understanding." He was careful when he dealt with the unpleasant items and either ignored them or barely touched on them. It covers the Roman invasion (55 B.C.) through a little beyond Queen Victoria's reign. An extremely valuable book that will entertain as it teaches.

IRL: 6th to 9th grade

Legends Every Child Should Know
Edited by Hamilton W. Mabie
(1906), Doubleday, Page & Co.New York. HB, 261 pgs.

What is a legend? According to Mabie they originated in church and centered around religious people and places. Usually they had some true facts combined with fiction which eventually led to an understanding that legends could be based on either a real person or an imaginary one. Mabie writes, "it throws light on the mind and character of the age that produced it...above all, it is interesting." Nineteen legends are presented here by authors such as Tennyson, Longfellow, and Hawthorne. Topics include Hiawatha, Beowulf, Sir Galahad and Rip Van Winkle. Primarily prose, it does include a little poetry.

IRL: 7th grade & above

Life of Greece, The
Will Durant
(1939) Simon & Schuster, New York. HB, 754 pgs.

This huge book is actually the second from Will Durant's *Story of Civilization* but he wrote it to stand alone as a complete unit. It covers a massive time frame from 9000 BC to AD 1104, however, The Rise of Greece chapter beginning on page 66 covers from 1000 to 480 BC. Durant provides thorough information on topics such as, the common culture, politics, trade, slavery, women, morals, schools, religion, books and philosophers. This book is extremely comprehensive and probably best appreciated by adults, Greek history buffs, or used as a reference tool in late high school.

IRL: 12th grade & above

Lincoln; An Illustrated Biography
Philip B. Kunhardt, Jr., Philip B. Kunhardt III & Peter W. Kunhardt
ISBN 0-679-40862-2 (1992), Alfred A Knopf, Inc., New York. HB, 415 pgs.

The most prominent and praiseworthy thing about this book is its photography and the credit goes to Frederick Hill Meserve. He was the grandfather and great-grandfather of the authors and left his collection to his descendants. Meserve committed himself to finding, identifying and preserving *every* photograph of President Lincoln. This book even has pictures of Lincoln's dog and books he personally owned. A very nicely done biography for those who want to know as much as possible about the sixteenth president.

IRL: 11th grade & above

Ludwig Van Beethoven
Edited by Joseph Schmidt-Gorg & Hans Schmidt
Library of Congress Number 70-100925 (1970), Deutsche Grammophon Gesellschaft mbH, Hamburg. HB, 276 pgs.

This beautiful, coffee-table style book is a great example of how history ought to be taught. Beyond being an outstanding and complete teaching on Beethoven's life, it includes many original facsimile documents and masterpiece portraits. These oil paintings include the people in power at the time, family members, scenery and architecture around which the composer lived. Many of Beethoven's original compositions with notes to friends scribbled in margins are fascinating to see. Thorough coverage like this will result in thorough retention for the student, not to mention a most enjoyable experience along the way.

IRL: 11th grade & above

Memoirs of Sir Walter Scott
J. G. Lockhart
(1890), Frederick Warner & Co., London & New York. HB,383 pgs.

This is an in-depth look at the life of Sir Walter Scott. It contains a beautiful portrayal of his daily life in Abbotsford in which you get the sensation you were there to see him ride by on his horse Sibyl Gray. He had many visitors including the King and it was said of him, "He was all along courted by the great world—not it by him." It also has many letters written to and from Sir Walter helping to authenticate the account. The font in my copy is extremely small and the content is very detailed making this a book for older children or adults.

IRL: 11th grade & above

Men of Achievement: Inventors
P. G. Hubert Jr.
(1893), Charles Scribner's Sons, New York. HB, 299 pgs.

Men of Achievement: Inventors
P. G. Hubert Jr.
ISBN 0-7661-0532-6 (1992), Kessinger Pub. Co, Kila, MT. (Ph. 406-756-0167), PB, 316 pgs.

Informative and well-written this book covers Franklin, Fulton, Whitney, Howe, Morse, Goodyear, Ericsson, McCormick, Edison, Bell and more. The preface promises to deal "with our great inventors, their origins, hopes, aims, principles, disappointments, trials, and triumphs, their daily life and personal character." The biographies are great and their inventions are explained and illustrated.

IRL: 7th grade & above

Men of Achievement: Men of Business
W. O. Stoddard
(1893), Charles Scribner's Sons, New York. HB, 317 pgs.

The men of business covered in this book include, Astor, Vanderbilt, Tiffany, Roach, Morton, Morgan, Field, Depew, Stewart, Armour, Claflin, Roberts, Pullman, Cooper, Field and Stanford. This preface claims to be "somewhat like a gallery, [presenting] the likenesses of the warrior, the statesman, the diplomatist, the artist, the pioneer, the adventurer, the inventor, the explorer, the organizer, the foreseer, and other types of businessmen whose success is beyond dispute." Each man is linked to a trait such as tenacity, originality or genius.

IRL: 7th grade & above

Men of Achievement: Statesmen
Noah Brooks
(1893), Charles Scribner's Sons, New York. HB, 347 pgs.

The statesmen featured in this book include, Clay, Webster, Calhoun, Benton, Seward, Chase, Lincoln, Sumner, Tilden, Blaine, Garfield and Cleveland. The criteria in choosing who would be in this book was based on whether their, "attainments in statesmanship were the result of their own individual exertions and force of character rather than of fortunate circumstances." Additionally, Brooks had the advantage of personally knowing many of the men in the above list making his insights very accurate.

IRL: 7th grade & above

Messages and Papers of the Presidents
Compiled under the Joint Committee on Printing
Bureau of National Literature, Inc., New York. HB, 509 pgs.

Because many educationalists agree that referring to original letters, documents and speeches helps bring life and accuracy to the study of history, I look for books like this one. I happened upon the 15th volume which mainly consists of papers and speeches by Theodore Roosevelt, however it begins with William Howard Taft which is concluding from the previous volume. Early in this volume is Roosevelt's Proclamation that the U.S. will set apart Thursday, the 24th of November to observe Thanksgiving Day. The best use for a book like this is to read from it—not through it.

IRL: 10th grade & above

Mornings on Horseback
David McCullough
ISBN 0-671-22711-4(1981) Simon & Schuster, New York. HB, 445 pgs.

This is a very detailed biography of Theodore Roosevelt. It begins in 1869, New York City, in the household of Theodore Roosevelt (our 26th President's father) whose father had given all five of his sons a house of their own. This president was a unique person with unique politics. He pursued a strenuous life, loved books, the outdoors and nature study. He was also a Harvard graduate who could not spell. The book also includes photographs beginning with Lincoln's funeral procession passing the Roosevelt house with Theodore and his brother Elliott watching from the window.

IRL: 12th grade & above

Our Empire Story; Stories of India and the Greater Colonies

H. E. Marshall, illustrated by J. R. Skelton
(1908), T. C & E. C Jack Ltd., London. HB, 493 pgs.

Marshall, who is my favorite historical author, attempted to explain in this book how the English Empire came to exist. His writing style is story-like and directed at the children's level, however, as an adult I learn and retain more from his work than any other sources. He begins with Leif, son of Eric the Red and his explorations, continues with Columbus and John Cabot until Sir Humphrey Gilbert declared New-found-land to be the possession of Queen Elizabeth. After thorough coverage of Canada (augmented with Canadian poetry) he moves on to Australia, New Zealand, South Africa and finally India.

IRL: 7th grade & above

Our Island Story; A History of England for Boys and Girls

H. E. Marshall, illustrated by A. S. Forrest
T. C & E. C Jack Ltd., London. HB, 557 pgs.

I love Marshall's books. In his introduction he writes, "this is not a history lesson, but a story book . . . remember, too, that I was not trying to teach you, but only to tell a story." The second chapter describes the invasion of the Romans and the book continues through every monarch until King George V and into the world war. He combines legend with fact and gives a thorough history in a friendly, helpful way that is truly a delight to read. This Charlotte Mason recommendation will make a great read aloud to grade school students or as independent reading for children between ages eleven and fourteen.

IRL: 6th grade & above

Our New Possessions
Trumbull White
(1898), J. S. Ziegler & Co., Chicago. HB, 676 pgs.

This book is really four books in one—it covers the Philippine Islands, Puerto Rico, Cuba and the Hawaiian Islands. Each account begins with the discovery, exploration and history of the original inhabitants. It is very descriptive and includes many black and white photographs. Eye witness accounts and actual letters of people from the times add depth and accuracy. Natural resources and climates are also described.

IRL: 7th grade & above

Our Sea Power
H. W. Household
(1918), MacMillan & Co., Ltd., London. HB, 179 pgs.

This book begins with the Mediterranean area and how the Phoenicians first ventured out into the Sea. It continues with the Greek and Roman exploration (eventually resulting in the invading of England) and it covers many peoples and cultures regarding their contribution to Sea travel. The purpose of the book is to explain how England won control of the Sea and why it was important to maintain that power. It was also hoped that the young readers would be inspired "to do the work in front of us, our daily work, with all our power." In other words, that the young would do their best and "show ourselves worthy of those who have died for us." Another book that the Charlotte Mason schools used.

IRL: 7th grade & above

Plato, Epictetus, Marcus Aurelius
Edited by Charles W. Eliot, LL.D.
(1909 & 1937), P. F. Collier & Son Corp., New York. HB, 345 pgs.

Plato took the philosophy of Socrates (born in 469 BC) and expanded upon it usually in a conversational format where Plato poses as the listener. This book includes Plato's *The Apology of Socrates*, *Crito* and *Phaedo*. It also contains *The Golden Sayings of Epictetus*, a first century Greek whose writings have either vanished or were never recorded. It was his follower Arrian who compiled Epictetus' teachings. He was known for finding happiness within relying not on externals. *The Meditations of Marcus Aurelius Antoninus* are included as well. Marcus, born in AD 121, was a Roman ruler who allegedly cared about the welfare of his people. He was so concerned about pleasing the population he agreed to their demand to execute Christians.

IRL: 9th grade & above

Plutarch's Lives, Vol. 1 & 2
Plutarch, Edited by Arthur Hugh Clough
ISBN 0-679-60008-6, Vol. 1, 0-579-60009-4, Vol. 2(1992), The Modern Library, New York. HB, 764 pgs. & 704 pgs.

Plutarch was born around AD 45 making him the oldest author featured in this book. His work was titled *Parallel Lives* and the point was to provide a biography of a prominent Greek man followed by one of a Roman man and finally to compare the two lives. Together, these two volumes supply fifty biographies—there are editions available with far less offered. Plutarch is often referred to as the original biographer and it's widely agreed upon that Shakespeare used some of his work as a starting point for his plays.

IRL: 12th grade & above

Queen Elizabeth
Katharine Anthony
(1929) The Literary Guild, New York. HB, 263 pgs.

Princess Elizabeth was born in 1533 to King Henry the Eighth and Queen Anne. Twenty–five years later she was Queen of England. This thorough book covers her entire life in great detail and reveals how dangerous it was to be born to a royal family. It has been said that "there was no respite from her birth and position" but Katharine Anthony writes that Elizabeth did not ask for one. She was an extremely devoted ruler and in the author's words, "Her reign was a marriage, and the nation was her child."

IRL: 8th grade & above

Scotland's Story; A Child's History of Scotland
H. E. Marshall, Illustrated by Skelton, Hassall & Crompton
T. C. & E. C. Jack, Ltd., London. HB, 428 pgs.

Caledonia, a little girl, asked Marshall to write "Scotland's Story for littler children like me." Rather than producing a tedious simplification he wrote 428 pages of the best history I've ever read. My family and I really enjoyed our time with this book, and even though it was written to children I like reading the story of William Wallace and Robert the Bruce from Marshall's viewpoint because of his writing talent. He does not apologize for including "golden threads of romance" as he recorded some folk lore in his history.

IRL: 6th grade & above

Stories From the History of Rome
Mrs. Beesly
(1878), MacMillan and Co., Ltd., London. HB, 189 pgs.

Mrs. Beesly was dissatisfied telling only fairy tales to her children. She wisely noted that the vocabulary in books such as *Plutarch* were beyond her young children. Deciding that it wouldn't hurt to experiment with simplifying the old tales from Rome she found the children not only enjoyed them but they requested them over and over again. This led to her publishing the work. As an adult I enjoyed the book and learned a great deal.

IRL: 5th grade & above

Stories of the French Revolution
Edited by Walter Montgomery
(1893), Estes and Lauriat Publishers, Boston. HB, 182 pgs.

This book starts with the death of King Louis the XIV and continues through to General Bonaparte. It is evident from its appearance that this is meant to be a children's book, however, the events described are brutal to say the least. There were many people killed during this era in French history and most of them had their decapitated heads displayed after their death. This is a great book because it makes the Revolution come to life, but use discretion as some descriptions are very detailed.

IRL: 7th grade & above

Story of Greece, The
Mary MacGregor, Illustrated by Robert Hodgson
(1959), (New Edition), Thomas Nelson and Sons Ltd., Edinburgh. HB, 328 pgs.

MacGregor is a gifted author and she starts this book on Greek history with mythology and ends it with the death of Alexander in 323 BC. She presents an easy to read story because of her narrative style (something I always look for in a book). I would recommend reading from it to younger children and having older children read it in its entirety. The index provides a way to look up a famous name and re-familiarize yourself with the details. I encourage you not to pass up a chance to buy any of her books—you won't be disappointed.

IRL: 7th grade & above

Story of My Life, The
Helen Keller
(1902), Doubleday, Page & Co., New York. HB, 465 pgs.

My copy of this book is called a special edition because it contains an account of Helen Keller's education, letters written by Miss Sullivan and Helen herself, plus it's illustrated. Keller was a lover of nature and literature. She had a thorough education in the classics which she read in English, French and German. The list of books she read include, *Greek Heroes*, Lamb's *Tales from Shakespeare*, Dicken's *A Child's History of England* , *The Arabian Nights*, *The Swiss Family Robinson*, *The Pilgrim's Progress*, *Robinson Crusoe*, *Little Women*, *Heidi*, *The Scarlet Letter*, and the *Iliad* all of which bring to mind the recommendations of Charlotte Mason.

IRL: 6th grade & above

Story of Rome, The
Mary MacGregor, Illustrated by Robert Hodgson
(1959) (New Edition), Thomas Nelson & Sons Ltd., Edinburgh. HB, 374 pgs.

This book opens with Roma's decision to burn the ship which had carried her husband, herself and others escaping Troy. The passengers had landed in Italy and the women found it pleasant and proceeded to carry out her plan. The following chapters are short but informative. MacGregor thought that this book might appeal to boys more than to girls due to the "terrible and cruel deeds, for the Romans were often pitiless." The bulk of the book deals with 753 BC to AD 14 and the exciting content will help bring ancient history to life.

IRL: 7th grade & above

Tales from Westminster Abbey
Mrs. Frewen Lord
Sampson, Low, Marston & Co., Ltd., London. HB, 119 pgs.

Westminster Abbey is the final resting place of people such as Chaucer, Shakespeare, Handel, Tennyson, Isaac Newton and the Kings and Queens of England. Mrs. Lord first describes how the Abbey was built and then she covers the layout of the interior. The rest of the book contains the tales— small entries explaining the significance of the people buried there. This book was used by Charlotte Mason schools.

IRL: 6th grade & above

Timetables of History, The
Bernard Grun
ISBN 0-671-74271-X (English Lang. version 1963), Simon & Schuster, USA. PB, 724 pgs. (Originally pub. in German in 1946)

This is a reference tool with a great layout that is easy to use. It begins with 5000 BC and my edition ends with 1990 AD. Throughout the book seven categories are offered: A. History, Politics; B. Literature, Theater; C. Religion, Philosophy, Learning; D. Visual Arts; E. Music; F. Science, Technology, Growth; and G. Daily Life. If you looked at 1971 as an example you would see at a glance that the U. S. was bombing Vietnam, women had been granted the right to vote in Switzerland, *Love Story* was written, Apollo 14 & 15 went to the moon, a tidal wave killed 10,000 people in Bengal, Charles Manson was found guilty of murder and the U. S. banned cigarette ads on T. V. However, there are 91 other entries listed for that year.

IRL: 8th grade & above

Tragedy of Leschi, The

Ezra Meeker

ISBN 0-939806-02-9 (1980), The Historical Society of Seattle and King County, WA.
PB, 259 pgs. (Originally pub. in 1905)

I'm a big fan of Meeker who had a substantial impact in Washington state, however he is also an important national hero due to his heroic efforts to preserve the Oregon Trail. In the 1850's Washington was being settled by Whites which of course resulted in many dealings with the rather mild-mannered local Native Americans. Very few murders or massacres occurred however Chief Leschi (for whom the famous Seattle neighborhood is named) was accused and tried for murder. Meeker believed in his innocence and wrote this book to reveal the true facts. Additionally, it provides an accurate picture of pioneer life and describes true accounts of fascinating historical events that Meeker witnessed.

IRL: 9th grade & above

Voices of American Homemakers

Edited by Eleanor Arnold

ISBN 0-253-12986-9 (1985), Indiana University Press, Indiana. PB, 295 pgs.

I absolutely love this book. Over two hundred interviews were conducted with women who were raising families from 1890 to 1940 with some entries dealing with the 1950's. Actual women tell their stories of life in rural America. Everything from childbirth to refrigeration is covered in these anecdotes that make for some of the most emotional reading I've ever experienced. The sheer ordeal of washing clothes and feeding the children (who were not always long for this world) will give you and your children a new appreciation for your life and for the homemakers that came before you. Highly recommended.

IRL: 7th grade & above

Wall Chart of World History, The
Edward Hull
ISBN 0-88029-239-3 (1988), Dorset Press, USA. HB, 15 pgs.

The advantage of this wall chart is that it can remain folded into its 17 x 12 inch book format or it can be mounted on a wall. When unfolded it measures 180 inches in length. I have chosen to keep mine in book form and when we need to refer to it we unfold it on the floor. Young children frequently struggle with concepts such as decades, centuries or millenniums and this kind of tool greatly helps them to visualize time frames. It covers 4004 BC to the late AD 1980's.

IRL: 6th to 11th grade

When Knighthood was in Flower
Edwin Caskoden
(1898), Grosset and Dunlap Pub., New York. HB, 359 pgs.

The lengthy subtitle of this book reads: "or, the Love Story of Charles Brandon and Mary Tudor the King's Sister, and Happening in the Reign of His August Majesty King Henry the Eighth." The author, who came from a long distinguished line of Caskodens, was a descendant of William the Conqueror. One of his ancestors, of the same name, created a memoir during the sixteenth century from which this book was written. This account is corroborated by Sir Edwin's contemporaries with few exceptions. Caskoden's goal was not to write a historical narrative but to provide "a picture of that olden long ago."

IRL: 8th grade & above

Women's Diaries of the Westward Journey
Lillian Schlissel
ISBN 0-8052-0747-3 (1982), Random House, New York. PB, 621 pgs. (HB available.)

There is no doubt that migration across our country was one of the biggest events in our history. This book uses actual diary entries and covers the years 1841 through 1867. The material is covered chronologically and has the heartfelt touch of a real person's account of the multifaceted aspects of the dangerous trip. Many old pictures are included, however there was very little photography done on the Oregon Trail due to the lack of cameras. Most of the photos are studio poses taken after a successful crossing in order to mail them back east to family.

IRL: 7th grade & above (uses a very small font)

Words of Our Nation
John Gabriel Hunt
ISBN 0-517-19004-4 (1993), Portland House, New Jersey. HB, 271 pgs.

This book contains original letters, speeches, poems and documents written by various presidents, authors, naturalists and poets. It covers the birth of the nation, the civil war, geography, the social conditions and many other issues. An absolute must read with all the accuracy original documents provide. This is an important addition to any library. Highly recommended.

IRL: 9th grade & above

Year 1000, The
Robert Lacey & Danny Danziger
ISBN 0-316-55840-0 (1999), Little, Brown & co., New York. HB, 230 pgs.

The subtitle to *The Year 1000* is, *What Life Was Like at the Turn of the First Millennium*. This is fun and informative reading. It's a look at the simple, yet short, life one would have lived in England during the year 1000. Much of it is based on the Julius Work Calendar which consists on twelve months on twelve pages—each chapter of the book covers a month. Clothing, farming, coins and historical figures are some of the many interesting topics covered.

IRL: 9th grade & above

Youth's Plutarch's Lives, The; For Boys and Girls
Plutarch, Edited by Edward S. Ellis, M. A.
(1895), The Penn Publishing Co., Philadelphia. HB, 237 pgs.

This paraphrased version of *Plutarch's Lives* has forty–eight biographies compared to the fifty in the adult version listed earlier. Each entry is abridged and the comparisons are omitted. It's quite common in the U. S. to not assign *Plutarch's Lives* until graduate school, but Charlotte Mason was unique in recommending adults read from it to younger children. She never backed down from this opinion, however she did ask the adult to censor certain violent portions for the children's sake. A version like this one does that for you while eliminating much of the old world vernacular.

IRL: 9th grade & above

Science & Nature

A Tree is Growing
Arthur Dorros, Illustrated by S. D. Schindler
ISBN 0-590-45300-9 (1997), Scholastic Press, New York. HB, 32 pgs.

This is a pretty book and it teaches leaf shapes, tree identification, sap production and root development. Mushrooms, birds, insects and rodents are included as well. It's so beautiful that it makes a good picture book for young children below the IRL. We all know children learn from picture books—once you begin using quality books like this one, your standards and theirs, will be raised past some of the inane books available at stores and libraries.

IRL: 4th to 5th grade

A Zoo for all Seasons
Smithsonian Exposition Books
0-89599-003-2 (1979), Smithsonian Exposition Books, USA. HB, 192 pgs.

This book is like visiting the zoo when you are unable to make the trip. In fact, it might be a great book to prepare students for such an excursion. Several authors and photographers collaborated with an apparent goal to be thorough. Not only are various animals and birds covered but they went to the extra work of covering zoo's histories, the process of acquisition and the personalities of zoo specialists.

IRL: 7th grade & above

Adventures of Mr. Mocker, The
Thornton W. Burgess
(1914), Grosset & Dunlap, New York. HB, 188 pgs.

Mr. Burgess (1874–1965) wrote many children's books featuring animal characters. This book has 26 chapters staring Sammy Jay, Bobby Coon, Peter Rabbit and Mr. Mocker. I don't consider Burgess' work to be indispensable but it is popular. I believe the best use for this book, also known as *Bedtime Story Book Series*, is for reading practice during those "hard to find enough books" years which usually fall after 2nd grade.

IRL: 3rd to 4th grade

Butterfly Book, The
Donald and Lillian Stokes
ISBN 0-316-81760-5 (1991), Little, Brown and Co., USA. PB, 8x11, 94 pgs.

These authors write an informative book, provide great photography and give people practical how-to recommendations they can actually use. They have many other books such as *The Bird Feeder Book, The Bluebird Book, Complete Birdhouse Book*, two *Wildflower Books* and *The Hummingbird Book* mentioned later in this section.

IRL: 8th grade & above

Chipmunks on the Doorstep
Edwin Tunis, Illustrated by the Author
0-690-19044-1 (1971), Thomas Y. Crowell Co., New York. HB, 70 pgs.

This book is almost worth its weight in gold and I approve of it so much that it always accompanies me to speaking engagements as my favorite example of a "whole book." It has everything going for it; first hand knowledge (and zeal) of the subject, passion (in both the text and illustrations), excellent writing and humor. Tunis and his wife attracted Chipmunks and observed them to the point of being able to illustrate and explain their eating habits, burrow details including the storage areas and escape holes, even their swimming ability. By the end you'll know and love "Chippy" as much as Tunis does.

IRL: 6th grade & above

Country Diary of an Edwardian Lady, The
Edith Holden
0-8050-1232-X (1977), Henry Holt., New York. HB, 186 pgs.

Holden did not have this most beautiful of nature diaries published. Instead her desire was to keep it completely private. No one seems to have been aware of it until several decades after her death. This 1977 edition is a facsimile of Holden's beautiful water color paintings, her poetry entries and her running diary of nature's daily changes. I highly recommend this book. It has gone in and out of print but there are ample copies to be had. In the sequel you'll find Holden's handwriting has been replaced by typeset font.

IRL: 7th grade & above

Exploring Nature with Your Child
Dorothy Edwards Shuttlesworth
(1952), The Greystone Press, New York. HB, 448 pgs.

Shuttlesworth founded and edited the *Junior Natural History Magazine* published by the American Museum of Natural History for nineteen years. The photography and illustrations are okay but it's the text that makes this book valuable. It is very detailed and covers fish, birds, animals, plant life, weather, constellations and more. This book is a great combination of instructional data and activities children can do and it is fairly easy locate through a book store or internet search.

IRL: 7th grade & above

Fairy-Land of Science, The
Arabella B. Buckley, Illustrated by J. Cooper
(1878), Edward Stanford, London. HB, 244 pgs.

Originally this information was presented to children in the form of ten lectures. The author was asked to convert the content into a children's book and the result is a beautiful blend of literary writing and scientific teaching. This really is the epitome of what the educator Charlotte Mason recommended. Buckley's other literary science book followed this one. This book is very valuable and rare (if you get a chance to buy a copy don't pass it up), I obtained my copy from England. IRL: 6th grade & above

Garden Crafts for Kids
Diane Roades
ISBN 0-8069-0999-4 (1998), Sterling Publishing Co., Inc., New York. PB, 144 pgs.

Rhoades choose *50 Great Reasons to get your Hands Dirty* as her subtitle for this book. She provides step by step, how-to directions for gardening by including helpful photos, text and diagrams on such things as how to construct a cold frame. After preparing the novice gardener with advice on soil, tools and design she gives craft and recipe ideas to use at harvest time. Even experienced gardeners will find this book inspiring to children whose enthusiasm and cooperation you'll want sustained all through the project.

IRL: 7th grade & above

Greenhead
Louis Darling
(1954), William Morrow & Co., New York. HB, 95 pgs.

I learned a lot about mallard ducks from this book. The text is interesting and the illustrations are good. The book has an elementary appearance at first glance but it really goes into detail without unnecessary or boring information that probably wouldn't be retained anyway. The anatomy covered includes bones, digestive organs, vision, muscles, and feathers. Other birds are discussed in relation to the mallard. This worked well as a read aloud in the area of science.

IRL: 4th to 6th grade

Handbook of Nature Study
Anna Botsford Comstock
0-8014-9384-6 (1939, renewed in 1967 & originally pub. 1911), Comstock Pub. Associates, Cornell University Press, New York. PB, 887 pgs.

Comstock, born in 1854, was a professor of nature study at Cornell. She was called a "scientific genius" and this work is often referred to as the Bible of nature study. I found it to be extensive and easy to use. The topics covered are: how to teach nature, birds, fish, amphibians, reptiles, mammals, insects, wild and cultivated flowers, weeds, crops, trees, rocks and minerals, soil, magnets, climate, water and astronomy. It serves as a teaching text and a field guide. The black and white photography is satisfactory but not beautiful by today's standards. Simply choose a section, read the text, do as many of the suggested activities as you want and augment with a modern photography book.

IRL: 7th grade & above

Hollyhock Days; Garden Adventures for the Young at Heart
Sharon Lovejoy
0-934026-90-4 (1994), Interweave Press, Inc., Colorado. PB, 95 pgs.

Sunflower Houses; Garden Discoveries for Children of All Ages
Sharon Lovejoy
1-883010-00-4 (1991), Interweave Press, Inc., Colorado. PB, 144 pgs.

Books do not get any more beautiful or enjoyable than these created by Lovejoy. It is not easy to write an "escape" book while providing practical, hands-on activities that you can actually do, enjoy and learn from. The hand painted artwork using the best inks available combined with an attractive layout makes these books outstanding. You'll find important gardening teaching and innovative ideas such as creating a flower bed in the shape of a butterfly or writing a child's name when you sow the seeds. Highly recommended.

IRL: 7th grade & above (Even though I chose 7th grade as the independent reading level my 5th grade daughter finds these books to be simple and pleasurable reading.)

Hummingbird Book, The
Donald and Lillian Stokes
ISBN 0-316-81715-5 (1989), Little, Brown and Co., USA. PB, 8x11, 89 pgs.

Beautiful photography and good solid teaching make this an important book. The authors are knowledgeable on their topic and have written many other books pertaining to nature. The writing style falls somewhere between literary and typical text book making it easy to read and understand. Topics include attracting, identifying and even photographing hummingbirds. IRL: 8th grade & above

Insect Man, The
Eleanor Doorly, Woodcuts by Robert Gibbings
(1936), Penguin Books, Great Britain, PB, 167 pgs.

Jean Henri Fabre (1823-1915) was a French author and naturalist who wrote ten volumes on entomology. Using over 30 of Fabre's "tales" and ultimately his very words Doorly shows us Fabre's village, school and lifestyle. Based on a true story of an English family who purposely set out to find out as much as possible about this entomologist, the scenery and insect knowledge come to life through their enthusiasm. This book is another great example of the rare "literary" science book.

IRL: 6th & above

Jack's Insects
Edmond Selous
HB, 183 pgs.

In this book Maggie and Jack have fallen asleep while looking at an entomology book. Similar to the *Alice's Adventures in Wonderland* premise the rest of the story takes place within a world where various species of butterflies, spiders, grasshoppers (all much larger than the children) appear and through conversation teach the little humans a lot about their environment and habits. For example, they attend a Katydid concert, talk with a Cicada and meet with insects who do not look like insects at all when they first encounter them. This book was used and recommended by Charlotte Mason and our family really enjoyed it.

IRL: 6th to 9thgrade

James Herriot's Treasure for Children
James Herriot, Illustrated by Ruth Brown & Peter Barrett
ISBN 0-312-08512-5(1992), St. Martin's Press, New York. HB, 252 pgs.

The exceedingly frequent requests from my children to read from this book caused us to finish the eight chapters in about eight days. You'll find each chapter is the perfect length for a read aloud sitting. The illustrations are far above average and make this a beautiful and outstanding picture book. The stories are good and interesting and you don't have to be an animal lover to enjoy them. (This makes a great gift, too.)

IRL: 5th to 6th grade

Life and Her Children
Arabella B. Buckley, Illustrated by Mr. Wilson & Dr. Wild
(1880), Edward Stanford, London. HB, 312 pgs.

In this book Buckley does not attempt to write another natural history book—instead she concentrates on the lower forms of life. Ordinarily we would not expect beautiful, eloquent writing with topics like sea-cucumbers and insects. However, this author has a gift that far exceeds average. I recommend combining this text with a current photographic book of undersea life such as, *Splendors of the Seas*, ISBN: 0-88363-958-0. As with Buckley's other book, buy it if you get the chance.

IRL: 6th grade & above

Lord God Made Them All, The
James Herriot
9-553-20558-7 (1981), Bantam Books, USA. PB, 373 pgs.

Scottish born veterinarian James Herriot decided to write his first book in his fifties and as you know he did not stop at one. His easy, comfortable writing style has earned him spots on the *New York Times* bestseller list, worldwide fame and his work has been portrayed on Public Television. I first read this book cover to cover in the 7th grade and enjoyed every minute of it. If you're having trouble locating literary science books or have an animal lover in your family then start with any of Herriot's books. IRL: 8th grade & above

Nat the Naturalist: A Boy's Adventures in the Eastern Seas
George Manville Fenn
(1906), A. L. Burt Co. Publishers, New York. HB, 335 pgs.

Nat is an orphan who lives with his uncle and spends a lot of time watching wildlife. He develops a taste for hunting and taxidermy while maintaining a respect for life and nature study. As he becomes a world traveler he encounters birds, fish and more that are described vividly.

IRL: 7th grade & above

Nature Journaling
Clare Walker Leslie & Charles E. Roth
0-58017-088-9 (1998), Storey Books, Vermont. HB, 181 pgs.

Nature diaries and journals are not new. Charlotte Mason advocated keeping them for several purposes. It helps develop observation and it's very fun. Leslie began nature journaling in 1978 and she has been committed to filling in an entire 92 page sketch book per year. They have become so precious to her that her intention is to grab them first in the event of a fire. I have experience with keeping these journals, but I learned much more from this book. The numerous ideas and beautiful sketchings make this book worth every penny.

IRL: 7th grade & above

Nature Writings of Henry David Thoreau
Henry David Thoreau

ISBN 0-681-21905-X (1996 edition), Tally Hall Press, Michigan. HB, 697 pgs. (A compilation printed under several publishers since 1849 to 1865.)

This is four of Thoreau's books combined into one volume. It consists of *A Week on the Concord and Merrimack Rivers, Walden, The Maine Woods* and *Cape Cod*. The first two were published in Thoreau's lifetime and the others were released posthumously and are based on travel experiences. The most well-known of course is *Walden* which has a separate entry. It's nice to have the bulk of Thoreau's work in one book.

IRL: 10th grade & above

Naturewatch; Exploring Nature With Your Children

Adrienne Katz

ISBN 0-201-10457-1(1986), Addison-Wesley Publishing Co., USA. PB, 128 pgs.

Naturewatch is full of activities to do with children. Sure, there's daisy chains, seed necklaces and pressed flowers but this book just keeps coming up with ideas. There are fun experiments for hands-on learning about insects, birds, trees, gardening and more. Another novel thing about this book, throughout there is light print for the teacher, parent or older child and dark print in boxes where the text is directed to children.

IRL: 9th grade & above (for the light print & 6th to 8th grade for the dark print)

Parables From Nature

Margaret Gatty

(1902), Thomas Y. Crowell & Co., New York.. HB, 114 pgs.

Parables From Nature

Margaret Gatty, Illustrated by Alice B. Woodward

(1921), G. Bell & Sons Ltd., Cambridge.. HB, 350 pgs.

Please note the page count difference in the above editions. The 1902 Crowell & Co. mentioned first is an abridged version which only offers one quarter of the original and has no illustrations. It is the one you will likely receive if you request an interlibrary loan. The 1921 edition is far superior with its beautiful illustrations and complete text. To obtain this one you'll need to check an out-of-print service and be specific about the version you're looking for. Gatty first published this book in 1855 and she wrote five other books. You'll find these parables to be scientifically accurate as she was careful to work with two scientists and has references to God and the scriptures throughout. Charlotte Mason used this book in her schools.

IRL: 7th grade & above

Sciences, The
Edward S. Holden
(1903), Ginn & Co., New York & London. HB, 224 pgs.

This book is subtitled, *A Reading Book for Children* and it is one of the science books recommended by Charlotte Mason. The topics include, Astronomy, Physics, Chemistry, Meteorology and Physiography (geography). The text is presented as children having a conversation with one another and they follow through with observation and experiments. However, the subject matter is varied and extensively covered. The illustrations are helpful (and include telescopic photographs of the moon) but more current visual aids could really enhance the teaching. This book could be used with any age group; as a read aloud for the younger child and as a remedial tool for the high school student.

IRL: 6th to 9th grade

Son of the Walrus King
Harold McCracken, Illustrated by Lynn Bogue Hunt
(1944), J. B. Lippincott Co., New York. HB,129 pgs.

This was the third animal/nature book for this author and it was used in school districts. His story begins with little Aivik's (the native word for walrus) babyhood in the Arctic. The habits and behaviors of the Arctic animals and birds are presented as the hero of the story makes his way to being king. The author's other books are titled *The Last of the Sea Otters* and *The Biggest Bear on Earth*. I don't recommend McCracken books as read-alouds, instead they are good for informative reading practice.

IRL: 6th to 8th grade

Splendors of the Seas
Norbert Wu
ISBN 0-88363-958-0 (1994), Beaux Arts Editions, HB, 252 pgs.

Wu decided to become a naturalist at the age of six. He became a marine biologist who has an extraordinary gift for photography. He has worked for Jacques Cousteau, the Smithsonian, Audubon, *National Geographic*, *Omni* and the PBS Nature series. This oversized book contains the most beautiful underwater pictures I've ever seen. It's a well rounded collection because Wu traveled the entire globe and he presents his pictures according to habitat such as Coral Reef and Deep Sea. Because the accompanying written text is exceptional this book far surpasses typical science books.

IRL: 7th grade & above

Squirrels and other Fur-Bearers
John Burroughs
(1875), Houghton, Mifflin Co., New York. HB, 149 pgs.

Burroughs wrote and read a lot. His favorite authors included Audubon, Emerson, Whitman and Matthew Arnold. Some have thought highly enough of his writing to group him with Thoreau. This book covers thirteen animals including raccoons, porcupines, skunks and wild mice. Burroughs writes in an informative yet friendly style that makes either silent or reading aloud pleasurable.

IRL: 6th grade & above

Strange Birds at the Zoo
Julia T. E. Stoddart, Illustrated by Margaret S. Johnson
(1929), Thomas Y. Crowell Co., New York. HB, 169 pgs.

When a child has a zeal for reading, keeping that child occupied with decent books can be challenging. A child's constant appetite for reading can be resolved while learning with this book. Mr. and Mrs. and Grandfather Peacock talk their way through the zoo introducing us to all of the other birds. This a good candidate for bedtime reading to young children.

IRL: 4th to 5th grade.

Walden; or, Life in the Woods
Henry David Thoreau
(1854), Holt, Rinehart & Winston, New York or New American Library, New York. PB, 250 pgs.

Walden is often printed with Thoreau's essay, *Civil Disobedience* which had far reaching influence upon well known people such as Mahatma Gandhi. Mainly, he believed in noncompliance or passive resistance when individuals disagreed strongly with their government. He lived out his philosophy by not paying certain taxes (to oppose slavery), spending a night in jail and moving to Walden's Pond (located on Emerson's property) to live a simple life. His descriptions of economizing, material possessions and immense time spent in nature have become classic reading.

IRL: 10th grade & above

Weather Book, The
Michael Oard
0-89051-211-6 (1979), Master Books, Arizona. HB, 80 pgs.

This is a Christian based "whole book" on weather with a somewhat textbook-ish format. While this is not a work of literature it's a fun and entertaining book. Climates, fronts, thunder, lightning, hurricanes, tornadoes and winter storms are among the topics presented. There are four pages of easy weather experiments your children can do at the close of the book.

IRL: 7th to 8th grade

Wild Animals I Have Known
Ernest Thompson Seton
ISBN 014-017005-7 (1987), Penguin Group. USA, PB, 358 pgs.

This particular title shows up in used book stores on a constant basis because it's been in print since 1898. The above mentioned ISBN is the currently available in-print facsimile of the antique version. Seton served in the Canadian government as a naturalist. He also helped found the Boy Scouts and was most famous for this book which he claimed were true stories. Some have felt they had no choice but to doubt the claim and some believe the author. In any case the stories, true or otherwise, cover wolves, crows, rabbits, dogs, foxes, horses and various birds.

IRL: 7th grade & above

Poetry

A Child's Garden of Verses
Robert Louis Stevenson, Illustrated by Jessie Willcox Smith

ISBN 0-517-12397-5 (1985 edition), Children's Classics, dist. by Random House, New Jersey. HB, 124 pgs. (Printed under several publishers since 1885.)

This work was generated, "From the sick child, now well and old." It's a well-known fact that Stevenson was a sickly child. My mother brought me his poetry as a sick young person myself and I spent days and days of my childhood absorbing every poem. He is, without a doubt, my favorite children's poet.

IRL: 4th to 6th grade

At Sundown
John Greenleaf Whittier, Illustrated by E. H. Garrett

(1890), Houghton, Mifflin & Co., New York. HB, 69 pgs.

Whittier originally published this poetry collection privately for his friends—two years and a few additional poems later this edition was released for the public. Whittier writes in an easy, gentle style providing non-poetry lovers a chance to dabble in this medium. Don't exert yourself looking for a first edition of this book, such as the above mentioned, as it may only be available through rare book exchanges. Any Whittier you come across, regardless of the format, will suffice.

IRL: 7th grade & above

Best Remembered Poems
Edited and Annotated by Martin Gardner

ISBN 0-486-27165-X (1992), Dover Publications, Inc., New York. PB, 210 pgs.

This is a very good anthology offering anywhere from one to nine works from sixty–four poets. The editor was not looking for the most "loved" or the "greatest" or even his personal favorites. His criteria was only if the poem would be remembered by "ordinary Americans." The poems are presented in alphabetical order according to author and a brief biography is included with each one. This is a good choice for the slightly older child.

IRL: 7th grade & above

Bird and Bough
John Burroughs

(1906), Houghton, Mifflin & Co., New York. HB, 70 pgs. (Originally pub. 1877)

Burroughs primarily writes on nature such as his work, *Squirrels and Other Fur-Bearers*. This is his only poetry collection and a large portion of the 34 poems are titled as names of birds. Many people look for poetic work that focuses on nature both in our day and in Burroughs. He answered requests he had received from the public and released this collection even though a critic had commented that his "readers could forgive me everything but my poetry."

IRL: 7th grade & above

Book of 1000 Poems, The

0-517-09333-2 (1993, prev. pub.), Wings Books, Random House. New York. HB, 630 pgs.

My favorite anthology of poetry suited to children. This one has the best indexes which include Titles, Classified Subject, First Lines and Authors— all of which come in handy at some time or another. It's a great collection at a great price.

IRL: 5th grade & above

Browning's Complete Poetical Works
Robert Browning

(1895), Houghton, Mifflin & Co., New York. HB, 1033 pgs. (Originally pub. 1887)

Browning was born in London in 1812. He, like so many other great minds of Great Britain, was buried in Westminster Abbey. He attended school and had private tutors but the bulk of his education was book-based. His father bought him copies of *Robinson Crusoe*, Milton, the Bible and attempted to instill a love for books. Elizabeth Barrett, his wife, was an invalid by time they met and it was because of her health they moved to Italy. I find it fascinating that two of my favorite poets were married to each other and as the man who sold me this book said, "Imagine the conversations they must have had."

IRL: 10th grade & above

Chief American Poets, The
Curtis Hidden Page, Ph. D.
(1905), Houghton Mifflin Co. USA. HB, 713 pgs.

A thorough collection of the following poets: Bryant, Poe, Emerson, Longfellow, Whittier, Holmes, Lowell, Whitman and Lanier all of whom Page considered to be chief. The poems are presented chronologically and dated with both the time of writing and publication. Brief biographical sketches are included on each poet relevant to his work. Page presents an unabridged collection with no boring criticisms or other needless dissections. Probably best appreciated by older students and adults.

IRL: 10th grade & above

Childe Harold's Pilgrimage
Lord Byron
(1885), Houghton, Mifflin & Co., Inc., New York. HB, 288 pgs.

The first half of this epic poem was published in 1812 and it was this work that secured his fame. His earlier work had been criticized and not as well received. I love Byron's writing style in *Childe Harold* and I could read it over and over again. I have read portions aloud to my children and whether or not they enjoyed it as much as I did, I know that were exposed to this genre and to some of the best poetry ever written.

IRL: 8th grade & above

Elizabeth Barrett Browning: Selected Poems

Introduced by Margaret Forster

0-8018-3754-5 (1988), The Johns Hopkins University Press, Maryland. PB, 330 pgs.

Elizabeth Barrett Browning is one of my favorite poets. The poems date from 1826 to 1862 and are presented in chronological order. Elizabeth was an extraordinary girl who wrote her first poem at eight and was published at fourteen. She was also able to translate Latin into English at a young age. She married poet Robert Browning at a time when her reputation was greater than his. Her 43rd *Portuguese Sonnet* written about her husband starts with, " How do I love thee? Let me count the ways."

IRL: 8th grade & above

Essay on Man and Other Poems

Alexander Pope

ISBN 0-486-28053-5 (1994 edition), Dover Publications, Inc., New York. PB, 97 pgs. (A compilation printed under several publishers since 1717 to 1735.)

Pope was born in 1688 and in addition to being an excellent poet he was a great satirist. His work varies from serious themes to the more lighthearted. My favorite is *The Essay on Criticism* where he spoke his mind on critics who in sheer moments can pass judgment over work years in the making. All essays included here are in the form of poetry. Dover Thrift Editions has more than 100 other books in this series, all unabridged, under $2.00 and nicely bound.

IRL: 10th grade & above

Favorite Poems of Henry Wadsworth Longfellow

H. W. Longfellow with introduction by Henry Seidel Canby

(1947), Doubleday & Co., Inc., New York. HB, 395 pgs.

Longfellow's poems have been published many times and in many styles and I see the evidence of this in nearly all the bookstores I visit. He was a New Englander born in 1807 to an affluent family and was a classmate of Hawthorne. Although I chose 9th grade independent reading level there are many poems suitable for young children to commit to memory such as *The Arrow and the Song, My Cathedral* and *The Village Blacksmith*.

IRL: 9th grade & above

Favorite Poems Old and New
Selected by Helen Ferris
ISBN 0-385-07696 (Trade), & 0-385-06249-4 (Prebound) (1957), Bantam Doubleday Dell Publishing Group, Inc., New York. HB, 598 pgs.

Every home needs a good poetry anthology and this is not only an exceptional one but easily obtainable. In addition to the great selections you'll find three indexes. There is the Index of Titles, First Lines and Authors. The table of contents provides subjects to find poems on particular topics such as patriotism, pets and families.

IRL: 5th grade & above

History and Rhymes of the Lost Battalion
"Buck Private" McCollum, Illustrated by Franklin Sly & Tolman R. Reamer
(1939), Bucklee Publishing Co., Inc., USA. HB, 161 pgs.

Buck Private's actual name was L. C. McCollum and this humorous yet accurate poetry was unanimously endorsed by the Post Commander and his men. McCollum was an amateur poet and knew it. His deep patriotism, love of country and sense of duty were undeniable. His realistic reactions to "killing men we've never seen" and questions like "have you been there, and if so what for?" cut through more like Vietnam War sentiments than the WW1 ones. McCollum finds humor amid the death and propaganda and there's a lot to be learned from his rhymes. My copy was from the fortieth printing (fairly abundant), I hope you can locate a copy and gain some insight on "The War to end all wars."

IRL: 7th grade & above

Lady of the Lake
Sir Walter Scott
(1830 edition), W. B. Conkey Co., Chicago. HB, 255 pgs. (Written in 1810.)

Scott, known for his historical novels was also a poet as we can see in his work, *The Lady of the Lake*. He turned down the position of poet laureate three years after writing this epic poem. If you want to expose your children to book length, narrative poetry (that rhymes!) and is beautifully written then I can think of no one more enjoyable to read than Sir Walter Scott. Best appreciated by older children and adults.

IRL: 9th grade & above

Nineteenth–Century Women Poets
Edited by Isobel Armstrong & Joseph Bristow
ISBN 0-19-818483-2 (1996) Clarendon Press, (Oxford University Press Inc.,) New York. PB, 826 pgs.

I have never regretted purchasing this book and I've found myself reading it time and time again. I find poetry to be refreshing reading when I need to "escape." The 102 poets are presented in chronological order (according to their birth dates) and a brief biography is included on each one. With a collection like this you will be able to choose favorite poets and then purchase their works. With any large collection of poetry you're bound to find the occasional "objectionable" line or subject and you may find yourself avoiding a few entries. However, with 826 pages there is plenty of great work to enjoy.

IRL: 10th grade & above

Robert Frost's Poems
Robert Frost
(1946) Pocket Books, Inc., New York. (Originally pub. by Henry Holt & Co., in 1930.) PB, 279 pgs.

Robert Frost: Selected Poems
Robert Frost
ISBN 0-517-07245-9 (1992) Random House, New Jersey. HB, 224 pgs. (Frost's first book was pub. 1913, his second in 1914 & third in 1915.)

Frost was born in San Francisco however he moved to New England as a boy. Later in life he and his wife lived in England. He won the Pulitzer Prize for poetry four times. Certainly not all of his work is nature related but he does lean in that direction. His two most memorable poems are, *Stopping by Woods on a Snowy Evening* and *The Road Not Taken*.

IRL: 7th grade & above

Stopping By Woods on a Snowy Evening
Robert Frost; Illustrated by Susan Jeffers
ISBN 0-525-40115-6 (1978) Dutton's Children's Books, New York. HB, 27 pgs.

This book features *only one* of Robert Frost's famous poems with delightful illustrations resulting in a young child's picture book. By using a child friendly format (which young audiences are accustomed to) the adult is able to present poetry that will entertain. This kind of introduction is preferable and will not cause an aversion to poetry, on the contrary it will help to develop a love for it. A great gift book.

IRL: 4th to 5th grade

Tennyson's Idylls of the King
Lord Alfred Tennyson
(1912), The MacMillan Co., New York. HB, 434 pgs. (Originally pub. between 1858 and 1885.)

Tennyson wrote poetry for over fifty years and was the poet Laureate after Wordworth's death. The Arthurian theme is evident from the titles of the poems included such as, *The Coming of Arthur, Lancelot and Elaine, The Holy Grail* and *Guinevere*. Tennyson also wrote patriotic poems like, *The Charge of the Light Brigade* and he was well-known for poetry on nature.

IRL: 9th grade & above

Art

Men of Art
Thomas Craven
(1931), Halcyon House, New York. HB, 524 pgs.

This is an extremely well-written biographical book covering twenty artists. It also covers regions and developments in chronological order which is helpful to the reader. A few black and white works of the artists follow the very enjoyable text. While *this is not* the book for great art prints, it offers the best biographies of artists I've found.

IRL: 9th & above

Miscellaneous

Book of Etiquette
Lillian Eichler
(1921), Nelson Doubleday, Inc., New York. HB, 288 pgs.

Etiquette fascinates me and I love to read books about it. This particular book covers manners, first impressions, engagements, weddings, funerals, introductions and all manner of correspondence. Etiquette also changes quickly and that's why a look back at former customs can be so interesting. While this is my favorite book on the topic you could probably find many others from the same era that would work well. The fun is in finding books several decades apart (including something current) and comparing the differences. IRL: 8th grade & above

Boy Who Held Back the Sea
Thomas Locker
ISBN 0-14-054613-8 (1987), Dial Books, New York. PB, 27 pgs.

Locker's books are far from ordinary picture books. Each page has a full sized, full-color reproduction of Locker's oil paintings. His talent is exceptional and his style follows Vemeer's interiors and his outdoor scenery is very well done. With the dramatic skies and beautiful detail the story comes to life.

IRL: 3rd grade

Early Christmas
Bobbie Kalman
ISBN 0-865505-003-1 (1981), Crabtree Publishing Company, New York. PB, 64 pgs.

I collect Christmas books and I also like Bobbie Kalman's books so every winter I put this one on the coffee table. I've read from it year after year and we all have it memorized. This one comes from her series called *Early Settler Life* in which each book begins with the word early. This is a very informative teaching on Christmas traditions starting with the American pioneers and a look at early cooking, decorating and gift giving helps bring perspective to current celebrations.

IRL: 5th to 6th grade

Home Crafts
Bobbie Kalman
ISBN 0-865505-505-X (1990), Crabtree Publishing Company, New York. PB, 32 pgs.

You will find I've recommended a total of four Kalman books altogether and this is the only example from the *Historic Communities* series which has eighteen books. Some other titles from this set include, *18th Century Clothing, A One-Room School* and *Games from Long Ago*. I like the teaching style in these books—information comes across in a friendly and retainable way. The photography really helps as well. Some topics covered in this book are, spinning, dyeing, weaving, quilting and rug, soap and candle making. IRL: 4th to 6th grade

India the People
Bobbie Kalman
ISBN 0-865505-211-5 (1990), Crabtree Publishing Company, New York. PB, 32 pgs.

Another great Kalman book, this one is from the *Lands, Peoples, and Cultures Series* of which there are at least twenty–two in total. The photography is greatly improved in this series and really sets this book apart from a boring "social studies" book. Home life, history, customs, poverty and a lot more are covered here. I used this book to acquaint my children with India after we began *A Little Princess*.

IRL: 4th to 6th grade

Magic Windows
Ernest Nister
ISBN 0-399-20773-2 (1980), Intervisual Books, Inc. California. HB, 12 pgs.

Merry Magic-Go-Round
Ernest Nister
ISBN 0-399-20946-8 (1980), Intervisual Books, Inc. California. HB, 12 pgs.

These two books are facsimiles from antique books. *Magic Windows* was originally published as *In Wonderland* in 1895. Six poems are used along with six revolving pictures. The scene changes when the child slides the ribbon about five inches. The advantage to purchasing a book like this is that you can actually use it with children whereas the antique equivalent should probably be kept out of the child's reach due to its potential value. These make good gifts and provide an enjoyable introduction to poetry for young children.

IRL: 2nd to 3rd grade

Mathematicians are People, Too

Luetta Reimer & Wilbert Reimer

ISBN 0-86651-509-7 (1990), Dale Seymour Publications, California. PB, 143 pgs.

Mathematicians are People, Too Volume Two

Ernest Nister

ISBN 0-86651-823-1 (1995), Dale Seymour Publications, California. PB, 144 pgs

Finding a literary math book is next to impossible but the closest thing you'll probably find is a biography of a mathematician's life. Each of these volumes covers fifteen mathematicians including their discovery. Their life spans begin at 636 BC with the closest to modern times being AD 1985. While it is not an in-depth view into these historical people, it is a very nice treat to add to a math curriculum.

IRL: 6th to 8th grade

Mexico the People

Bobbie Kalman

ISBN 0-865505-215-8 (1993), Crabtree Publishing Company, New York. PB, 32 pgs.

This is the second and last example from Kalman's series social study works called *The Lands, Peoples, and Cultures Series*. The author starts with the ancient civilizations such as the Olmecs, Zapotecs and Aztecs helping children to see the cause of diversity in Mexico. Population explosions, family, clothing and all aspects of culture are covered here. As always with this author the end result is a well balanced book loaded with retainable information and great photography.

IRL: 4th to 6th grade

Travel Pictures

Presbyter Ignotus, AKA William Harman van Allen

(1912), The Young Churchman Co., Wisconsin. HB, 239 pgs.

This book was compiled from letters written while the author was traveling in Europe. About these letters, he writes, "[I] scribbled in country inns by candlelight, in the green privacy of ancient forests . . . [I'm] only asking the reader not to complain because he finds the result neither a Baedeker nor a scientific treatise." This author makes you feel as though you've accompanied him in his travels. His enthusiasm is evident and that is one thing we should look for when we assess any book—honest enthusiasm.

IRL: 8th grade & above

What Jane Austen Ate and Charles Dickens Knew
Daniel Pool
ISBN 0-671-88236-8 (1993),Simon & Schuster, New York. PB, 416 pgs.

Have you ever wondered about the many mysterious pastimes, currency, articles of clothing and customs casually mentioned in English literature? Pool provides a fascinating and page-turning revelation of the social order, daily life and even whist. Find out the qualifications of a baroness, countess or a lady and enjoy yourself while you do. Following the text is a handy glossary for quick reference to hundreds of unfamiliar terms. I literally could not put this book down and have reread it many times. Great for adults who have begun to delve into nineteenth century English literature and children of all ages will enjoy read-alouds from this book.

IRL: 8th grade & above

Where the River Begins
Thomas Locker
ISBN 0-14-054595-6 (1987), Dial Books, New York. PB, 27 pgs.

As mentioned before Locker's books are far from ordinary picture books. In this one Josh and Aaron live near a river and decide to find its origin. Their grandfather escorts them on a camping trip to follow the river where they find its source is a pond. It's the beautiful oil paintings that make this book worth owning and reading over and over again.

IRL: 3rd grade

Biographies

Drawn From New England; Tasha Tudor
Bethany Tudor
ISBN 0-399-20835-6 (1979), Philomel Books, New York. HB, 96 pgs.

Tasha Tudor was a very unique person with an equally unique lifestyle. She was born in 1915 and actually lived an entire lifetime in that era by shunning modern conveniences and cooking meals with a wood burning stove. She spun, wove and sewed her own dresses, farmed, kept livestock, even made butter in old fashioned decorative molds. She was a good mother and always celebrated birthdays and holidays with elaborate, self created, traditions. She's most well known as an artist who illustrated many children's books. This biography written by her devoted daughter tenderly explains this mysterious woman with great text and good photographs.

IRL: 8th grade & above

Dylan Thomas: a biography
Paul Ferris
ISBN 0-8037-1947-7 (1977), The Dial Press, New York. (Originally pub. in Great Britain by Hodder & Stoughton) HB, 399 pgs.

I'm easily entertained by biographies—I'll read one on literally anybody. I have a particular interest in Dylan Thomas and an affinity for anything or anyone who is from Wales. Ferris, also Welsh, was born "fifteen years after Thomas and a mile from his house." His years of research are apparent in his writing—of course his subject had the unusual experience of being famous in his own lifetime and left behind many eyewitnesses who saw him live it. Ferris has authored at least fifteen books and his writing abilities are excellent.

IRL: 11th grade & above

Music

A Taste for The Classics
Patrick Kavanaugh
ISBN 0-917143-29-9(1993), Sparrow Press, Tennessee. HB, 244 pgs.

The world of classical music contains many terms that leave most adults and students feeling somewhat ignorant. If you've ever wanted to know the difference between a symphony and a suite, or how an orchestra compares with chamber music, this is your resource. The author explains seven genres, includes biographical information and influences on the composers, provides a list called *Your First Thousand Pieces* and an excellent glossary. The teaching is very complete and well presented.

IRL: 8th grade & above

How Music Grew
Marion Bauer & Ethel Peyser
(1925), G. P. Putnam's Sons, New York. HB, 647 pgs.

How Music Grew is subtitled; *From Prehistoric Times to the Present Day*, meaning up until 1925. Starting with "primitive" people groups from the prehistoric times and progressing chronologically through the major cultures Egyptians music is described as having, "whole steps and half steps, covering several octaves, not unlike ours." While presenting the entire history of music many biographies are included on well-known people such as Bach, Beethoven and Wagner. The only omission is a purposeful one of excluding the singers. My family learned a lot from this nicely written book.

IRL: 9th grade & above

Spiritual Lives of Great Composers, The
Patrick Kavanaugh
ISBN 0-917143-08-6 (1992), Sparrow Press, Tennessee. HB, 119 pgs.

Kavanaugh provides brief biographies on Handel, Bach, Haydn, Mozart, Beethoven, Schubert, Mendelssohn, Liszt, Wagner, Dvorak, Ives and Stravisnsky in order of their life-spans. Each biography is followed by a concentration of the composer's work complete with suggested selections for listening. I recommend reading *from* the book rather than straight through for better comprehension.

IRL: 7th grade & above

Appendix
Scope & Sequence

The following is meant as a guideline for those who would like to follow or occasionally consult the general educational scope and sequence of the United States. I've studied many of these over the course of twelve years and this will serve as a conglomeration of what I've seen.

There are differences among the many scope and sequences across the country, however they do follow a pattern. Two I've recognized repeatedly is the alternating Eastern hemisphere studies one grade level then covering the Western hemisphere the next, on a continuous rotation. Sometimes that is combined with alternating between U. S. history and ancient history. The other is in the area of science. This field is broken into three parts, life science, earth science and physical science. The pattern is to primarily cover one per school year, move on to the next the following year and then continuously repeat the pattern with advancing material.

Classroom teachers have to follow a scope and sequence in order to pass on graduates to the next grade level. It is necessary so that the end result is a high school graduate who has supposedly covered the basic elements of education.

Parents of classroom students will have children following a course of study such as the following. These parents can choose books and literature that augment what their students are covering in any given year or even choose contrasting materials to help broaden their child's views.

Home educators have the luxury of choosing when to cover nearly everything. Many target something like biology or geology and cover that as a family regardless of the varying age levels in the home. Some will cover all the subjects all the time but choose one subject as the priority for the year such as home economics or Shakespeare. As different families choose different educational philosophies they also vary in how closely they want to follow what the local schools are doing year by year. A local scope and sequence is easily obtained simply by asking for one at the local school. Another option is to consult the many catalog companies to see what they think are the appropriate topics grade by grade.

One more thing to keep in mind. Skills differ from educational areas. Mathematics, hand writing and reading are examples of skills. Other topics are much more subjective—history, art, etc. For this reason, the following lists represent general terms without pinpointing exact content. I compiled it as a helpful tool for those who have repeatedly asked for such a list, and as possible way to observe a grade level and then to select books that compliment your child's grade level.

Kindergarten

Language Arts
  Letter recognition
  Letter formation
  Phonics
  Being read to and
    interaction about the subject

Science
  Animals, farm and zoo
  Plants, trees, leaves
  Easy astronomy

Math
  Numeral recognition
  Counting
  Shapes
  Size differentiation
  Easy measurement
  Simple more-than,
  less-than

First Grade

Math
  Numerical recognition to 100
  Number lines
  Easy addition and subtraction
  Beginning place values, the
    meaning of zero
  Shapes and measurement
  Calendars and clocks
  Simple fractions
  Coin recognition and counting

Science
Animals and environments
Plants (seeds and seedlings)
Solar System

Language Arts
  Direct reading
  Sight words and phonics
  Alphabetizing
  Simple punctuation
  Handwriting practice
  Easy spelling
  Creating sentences

Magnets
Birds
Seasons
Solids and liquids

Second Grade

Language Arts
Silent Reading
Punctuation use and recognition
Capitalization
Handwriting practice
Simple letters and composition
Synonyms and homonyms
Spelling
Dictionary skills

Science
Animals: extinctions, defense
  reproduction, food chain, habitats
Planets and Constellations
Weather & Climate
Water cycle

Math
Numeral recognition to
  one thousand
Place values to 1000
Easy fractions
Beginning decimals
Charts and graphs
Counting by two's,
  five's, ten's
Beginning multiplication
  table
Geometry

Gravity
Gases

Third Grade

Language Arts
Silent and oral reading
Paragraphs
Punctuation practice
Writing stories and poems
Antonyms
Dictionary practice, pronunciation
  marks and alphabetizing to the
  third letter
Cursive handwriting

Science
Energy and electricity

History
Native Americans
Explorers and Pioneers of
  the New World

Mathematics
Multiplication table
Geometry
Metric System
Rounding
Roman numerals
Negative numbers
More fractions

Orbit
Desert animals and plants
Simple geology
Arboretums and aquariums
Compass

Forest animals and plants
Flowers
Sea animals and plants
Machinery

Fourth Grade

Language Arts
Research reading
Outlining and note taking
Encyclopedia practice
Written narrations (summarizing)
Play (dramatically) reading
Continued practice in cursive
  and spelling

Math
Writing numbers with words
Multiplication through the twelve's
Averages
Seconds, minutes
Decimals and fractions
Mixed numbers
Division
Subtraction to the seventh place value
Multiplication by three digit numbers

History
Local State History

Science
Human anatomy
Oceanography
Universe
Pollution
Insects
Reptiles
Plant structure
Scientific method

More Roman numerals
Measurement
Geometry

Fifth Grade

Language Arts
Grammar, parts of speech
Characterizing literature
Thesaurus

History
United States History:
Colonization
Exploration

Plurals
Bibliographies
Library skills
Continued dictionary work

Math
Decimals to the thousandths
Fraction, decimal conversion
Words problems
Continued work with mixed
  numbers
Continued work with graphs

Early Settlers
Pioneer Life
Constitution
Declaration of
  Independence
Revolution

Science
Cells and bacteria
Adaptations
Space exploration
Scientific classification
Photosynthesis
Fish
Electrical conduction
Beginning chemistry

Sixth Grade

Language Arts
Root words, suffixes and prefixes
Continued grammar
Vocabulary advancement
Writing practice with journalism
Creative writing
Writing style classification
Continued note taking and skim
  reading

Science
Scientific theory
Nuclear and solar energy
Human nutrition
Continued astronomy

Math
Calculators
Fraction multiplication
  and division
Percent
Angles
Continued work with
  conversions

History
Roman History

Molds, algae and fungi

Seventh Grade

Language Arts
On-Line researching
Atlas work
Cont. grammar and sentence structure
Foreign language if not covered earlier
Oral presentations
Poetry
Short stories

Science
Earth Science/Geology
Conservation and ecology
Genetics

History
Greek
Roman
Renaissance

Math
Formulas
Making graphs
Business math
Infinite numbers
Prime numbers
Square roots
Continued
    geometry

Microscopes and
laboratory work

Early Eastern Hemisphere:
Both World Wars
Middle Ages

Eighth Grade

Language Arts
Advanced grammar
Business letters
Report and research papers
Biographies
Continued foreign language

Math
Mastery of basic mathematics

Science
Life science/biology
Classification
Human reproduction
Chemistry
Periodic table
Geology

History
United States history from

or Pre-algebra
Business Math

colonial life to the Civil
War
Geography / Map Skills

Ninth Grade

Language Arts
Research reports
Proofreading/editing
Journalism
Keyboarding
Speech writing/
  oral presentations
Debate
Poetry
Advanced dictionary work

Math
Algebra
Investment math
Banking
Taxes

Science
Earth science / geology
Chemistry / atoms and molecules
Technology

History
Local state history or Early U. S. government or Pacific Rim studies

Tenth Grade

Language Arts
Literature, American and
  global
Literary criticism
History of language and
  alphabets
Term papers

History
Eastern Hemisphere
China
India

Math
Geometry
Symbolic logic
Introduction to trigonometry

Science
Life science / biology
Ecosystems
Genetics
Nutrition
Cells and microscopic life

Middle East
Africa
British monarchies
The French Revolution

Eleventh Grade

Language Arts
Literature
Advanced vocabulary
Communication
Editorial writing
Advertising
Term papers

Math
Algebra II or Trigonometry

Science
Chemistry

History
United States History
From colonization to WW II

Twelfth Grade

Language Arts
Shakespeare
Theater
Tragedies and comedies
Book Reviews
English literature
19th Century literature
Periodicals
Bibliographies

Math
Advanced algebra or Calculus or
 pre-calculus
Computer science math

History
United States Government and/or
world problems

Science
Physics

For more homeschooling products
and titles by Catherine Levison,
visit our website at

www.championpress.com